STO

ACPL ITE
DISCARDED

S0-CBG-945

Decades—
Lifestyle Changes in Career Expectations

DECADES—

Lifestyle Changes

in

Career Expectations

Edith M. Lynch

amacom

A Division of American Management Associations

Library of Congress Cataloging in Publication Data

Lynch, Edith M
Decades: lifestyle changes in career expectations.

Includes index.
1. Vocational guidance. 2. Occupations.
3. Success. I. Title.
HF5381.L786   650.1'4   80-65703
ISBN 0-8144-5603-0

First Printing

With affection and appreciation, this book is dedicated to my family, my bosses, my subordinates, and my many friends in management. Special thanks to my husband, Peter, my daughter, Carlyn, and her husband, Peter, and to Clara Kushins, who put up with me for 18 years.

FOREWORD

Individuals are in rapid transition with regard to career attitudes and expectations. This book reflects those dramatic changes. The author shares her own personal experiences and anxieties and analyzes the experiences of 125 other executives.

The book brings into focus the risks involved in job changes and the security of staying put. It identifies the responsibility that the individual must assume for career choices and success. This is balanced against those things that companies are doing today to provide career counseling and guidance.

There is the opportunity to benefit from learning about many experiences of both successes and failures. These shared career experiences will allow the reader to reflect on his or her own progress to date and then to engage in personal career goal-setting and planning. The book suggests ways to avoid wasting human talents, in terms of time, potential, and opportunity. The individual must be willing to take certain risks in order to avoid a later feeling of regret over "what might have been."

Although the material recognizes a changing human environment, it also exposes the underpinning and family support needed for success. It highlights the importance of the unchanging values of appropriate work ethics and morality, which are essential to career success.

By dividing the life span into decades, the writer provides insights into the movement from one stage to another. In a sense, the reader is able to climb one side of the mountain to middle age from one plateau to another and then with increased age begin to descend on the other side in like manner. The writer's personal feelings and experiences are reinforced and made even more meaningful through the excellent reporting of survey results.

Although biographical in part, the book provides a broad variety of experiences. The material is both interesting and readable. It should provide valuable benchmarks for all individuals who are interested in analyzing their own careers and for those managers who must provide career counseling and systems for others.

Ray L. Killian
Vice-President and Director
Personnel, Operations, and Public Relations
Belk Stores

CONTENTS

1

The Situation Today—

Surveying the Territory

Over 98 million Americans are working. Of those, approximately 12 million are in administrative or management jobs. Today, work is an important portion of millions of people's lives. Many workers in management are happily progressing up the ladder in the traditional Horatio Alger fashion, but many others are caught in the dead-ends of unhappy and unproductive positions. Today's management field is tough; it's competitive and you must be agile to survive. The journey from youth to retirement is like a circuitous route through a mine field. Reaching the top in any profession means climbing the ladder of success and not hitting a rotten rung.

I have investigated today's management field and have found interesting and exciting views of how it looks to individuals at various periods of their lives. To learn how successful managers have met the challenges that the modern work world presents, I prepared and distributed a questionnaire* that explored their attitudes and opinions about personal risk, success, failure, changing jobs, and

---

*The questionnaire appears at the back of the book.

other issues. This book is based on the insights gleaned from 125 completed questionnaires, from over 25 in-depth interviews, and from my own observations of the management scene during the past 45 years. Although the book reflects the experiences of those who are and have been successful, that does not mean I am unaware of the tragedies that occur because of mistakes, failing health, or poor management practices. This book is more or less a survival kit, which I hope will provide some clues about why the management process works so well for many people. I am grateful to the managers who shared their experiences with me and thereby helped shape these insights.

Today is a time of ever-expanding opportunities, of specializations, of mergers and acquisitions (in which some of the strong as well as the weak fall by the wayside). It's a time when opportunities for education and training offer the ambitious individual more tools to work with than at any other time in history. It's a time of restlessness and of yearning. It's a time of change, when "new" breakthroughs quickly become obsolete.

Unlike workers from the old school, to whom the job came first and who subjected their families to moves and countless inconveniences, today's workers examine how a job should fit into the lifestyle of an individual and the family. In general, there is no longer the intense loyalty to an individual company; when such loyalty does exist it's usually because the company provides an opportunity to expand and to use one's talents. The seven-year itch (or, in the case of younger executives, the three- or four-year itch) is just as common as ever. In a national survey reported in *Psychology Today* (September 1977), two-thirds of the 23,000 readers polled indicated they would change occupations within the next five years. However, that article also reported that money and benefits are not enough to entice people to move. They need job satisfaction and a place to learn and grow, and want to be able to set their own pace and hours.

Life in the 1980s for up-and-coming managers is characterized by "I intend to make my first million by the time I'm 30," or, "You should double your salary within the first five years of graduation." Still another quote from the young eager executive: "You should earn as many thousands of dollars each year as you have years in your life." In other words, you should be making $20,000 when you are 20, and $65,000 when you are 65. In the middle years you'll hear, "I had to move out to move up," "I'm tired of not running my own show," or, "I thrive on responsibility—lead me to it." Even toward the end of a working career, people are planning their next step. More and more are risking job changes at 55, 60, and even 65.

How do the managers of today differ from the managers of 20, 15, 10, or even one year ago? There are tomes written on this subject, but here are some obvious answers: The workforce is better educated than ever before—the manager of today usually has at least one degree and many have more. The choice of jobs and opportunities available to young workers is a continual source of amazement to many of us. The woman of today, for example, can be an architect, a doctor, a company officer, a wage expert, a company lawyer, or a manager of the human resources of her firm. To the educated young man or woman, the job openings are exciting and numerous, and are often geared to his or her particular talents. Even in the smallest firms, international operations offer tremendous opportunities for the individual who is well versed in languages and is technically skilled.

The frenetic pace at which technologies change could

overwhelm the unwary, but it offers challenges for the geniuses of today and tomorrow. We also need the men and women who keep everybody glued together, the people who help steer others to the right path and encourage workers to develop their talents. The manager of human resources is the hope of the future in bridging the gap between technological and social know-how.

The work world, in other words, provides an exciting, challenging, innovative, and rugged environment in which most of us spend over half of our waking lives. Yet, is the upward journey free of perils? Is there a path through the jungle? Is there a carefully planned procedure? Will you be able to foresee all the dangers and pleasures of new and supposedly better jobs? What if you had blinders on—could you back out and return to a quiet little nook? Management is not for the fainthearted or the weak. If you make a mistake and take the wrong job, if you lose one that you thought was solid, or if you have plain, old-fashioned bad luck, there may be a few executives who will pick you up, dry your tears, and wish you well. But most are too busy with their own careers to support a faltering fellow-employee.

On the other hand, if you are wary, if you look before you leap, and if you meet each new challenging job with gusto, then the journey can be a wonderful, exciting adventure. As one executive put it, you must plan your course to "be careful it's not your head bobbing in the wake."

Can we learn from our experiences and pass along information that will be helpful to others facing similar challenges in their careers? I hope this book will help you plot your own path through your work life by giving you an awareness of the hazards of corporate life and by showing how to watch for the "green signals" that help you utilize your talents to the utmost. It's not an easy journey, but it can be an exciting and fulfilling one.

Management "Types"

My own working experience of 45 years has provided me with a ringside seat from which to observe the vagaries of the working world. I began as a schoolteacher in Ohio, I was shaken out of complacency by World War II, and I've been in the management arena ever since. As a woman working in that field long before ERA, it behooved me to move out in order to move up. I began in management as a wage analyst for the Bureau of Labor Statistics; my most recent position was vice-president for personnel of the National Retail Merchants Association. Like most other executives, I felt the seven-year itch, and have held six interesting management positions since I left the teaching field.

Throughout my career, I've come in contact with all sorts of workers. The characters described below grace today's management scene—I am sure many of them will be familiar to you.

○ There's Joe, the young executive-trainee, who's eager to please, full of vim, trustful, and respectful. He's a well-educated graduate of one of our fine universities who wants to learn and wants to get to the top—and fast. As one young fellow told me recently, "I want to make a million dollars by the time I'm 30."

○ Joe's female counterpart is Mae. Beautiful, well groomed, also well educated, Mae is often trained in a field that didn't exist when we older people were in school. She, too, is anxious to please and ambitious. She's sure she can manage her personal life, including a family, and plans not to marry until she is 30. She is often a little more aggressive than Joe because she's heard that women can have a rough time in management. Both Joe and Mae are beautiful people, but two out of four people like them will leave their first job within three years.

○ Poor Ed is in his forties and the management world has dismissed him from its hallowed halls. He is whipped, and he's sometimes embittered toward his last company and the world in general. He is well informed in his field and is trying desperately to regain his foothold. He used to be an ambitious young man with a dream, and can't figure out what happened in the past 20 years. The Eds who stay on the payroll are passed over for promotion, and nine times out of ten they are nonproductive and hopeless as bosses.

○ Nellie is the 40-year-old executive who has made it. She is sure of herself, makes the right decisions involving herself, her subordinates, and her company with speed and dexterity. She is healthy, bright, and still on the way up. She is innovative and is called in for decisions involving major company policies. In her age bracket she still is a few management steps behind her successful male counterpart, because opportunities at the corporate level have only recently really opened up for women. Although she may be smarter than the man who supervises her, there is no ill-will or jealousy on her part. She is married, with a successful husband and a couple of well-adjusted children.

You could pick a hundred male counterparts to Nellie, ranging anywhere from 30 to 55 years old. It seems that young people with the smarts are getting to the upper levels of management at a much earlier age than they used to.

○ Willie is 55. He has a good job that he thinks is safe.

His answer to the young bucks and the women who work for him is, "We've always done it this way." In other words, don't rock the boat. He's a yes-man to his superiors. His division is moribund, his subordinates are unhappy because they see no place to go, he is ignored when top management decisions are involved, he has lost his nerve and will seldom try anything new.

○ Jack is 62, has a clear mind and a bit more experience than Nellie, who's 40. His decisions are just as much on the beam as they were when he was younger. He often suggests new ways of doing things and is excited about developing the talent in his company. He is generous in his praise and goes out of his way to see that credit is given to those who deserve it.

○ Finally, there is poor old Sue, who, at 64, is really old. She has no new ideas, and dreams primarily of what she will do when she retires. She spends much of her time telling her fellow employees about her dire physical ills.

Why are some people successful and others failures? Can we learn from others or are we slated to a predestined path from which there is no deviating? Are we so weighed down with troubles, financial or otherwise, that we no longer see the oncoming years with any kind of eagerness? Have we survived the corporate jungle?

Hazards

Often the difference between success and failure is the recognition that there are danger spots. There are certain signals that say, "Stay clear of this sink hole," or, "Take a detour around this rocky road," or, "Catastrophies lie ahead—beware." Here are just a few red flags you should be alert to in today's management world. You can probably add to the list, and later in the book we will examine these in more detail.

First, do you really fit the specifications of the job? Many people lead a life of quiet desperation because they are in the wrong job. During World War II, the psychologist was sometimes in the first line of battle, the scholar was in the mortar platoon, and the budding doctor was out killing. Talk to any old soldier and he'll tell you many stories of misplacement. Yet, together those men won the war. Management, too, bumbles along; but when talents and jobs coincide, that is when mountains are moved.

Second, are you promising more than you can deliver? That can get you into trouble. The 1980s are a time of high job offers. An incumbent is often bypassed for a "genius" from elsewhere. If you are that genius and are being enticed by an offer of twice what you are receiving now—beware. If the pay is twice as good, chances are you'll have to perform twice as well. Too often, the job is not what was promised or when you arrive the management team that hired you has shifted elsewhere. There's no guarantee that the position you accepted is really what was promised, or that the team you hoped to work with is still intact.

Then there are those things beyond your control—mergers, for example. No matter what is said, there is no room for two vice-presidents of industrial relations. Mergers are supposed to sharpen management know-how, but too often, capable people are lost in the shuffle. Or, your company may go out of business. Be alert for signs of trouble, or you may go down with the ship. As one executive said, "I stayed in because I just couldn't believe that this 200-year-old company would fail." It did, and a capable middle-aged executive is on the beach. If you hold a responsible position in a company that gets in trouble, you'll be tarred with the same brush. Companies that fail dump many executives on the market with their names tainted.

Financial impropriety and scandal are real hazards of today's work world. If you abuse your expense account (one executive financed his honeymoon on his expense account) word usually gets around fast, and you'll find it hard to land your next job.

There are other danger signals, too. If your appraisal is consistently bad or if your boss lets you know that he thinks you are not doing a good job, don't wait until you get fired. If you can beat the ax, you will be in better shape for job hunting. And if you spare your boss the miserable tribal dance of firing you, you might even end up with a good reference.

Watch out for the few "rats" found in every office. They're the ones who would step on their mothers to move ahead. They are typically gossips, are ruthless, and are out to get anyone who challenges their turf. They are the kind who tell a peer's supervisor: "Don't you think poor old Joe is slipping? I guess he's drinking too much and his work is showing it." Almost any management scene has at least one person like this. Beware of him or her. They'll smile at you while they twist the dagger in your back.

The incompetent supervisor will drive a capable executive out of the company faster than any other factor. The squelcher of ideas, the don't-rock-the-boat boss, the idea-stealers, and the superior air of an inferior mind drive many executives to write a new resume. This same boss wants every job done *his* way, and is most reluctant to give credit when it is due. Avoid him. Not all supervisors are like that and there are opportunities elsewhere.

Still another danger is counting on someone from the outside of your own organization to save your job for you. For example, if your golf partner is a friend of the president of your company, you may think that a word from him could help your situation. Or, if you work for a trade association, you may be inclined to depend on assistance from outside executives to whom you have provided a service. They won't be able to help, however, if your own management has already decided that things are not working out. Well-meaning outsiders often don't understand the nuances of your trouble. Your current management doesn't want to be told from the outside how to run the show. Many an executive has hastened his or her own departure by depending on well-meaning, high-placed people from the outside.

As we progress further into the book we shall find other dangers that individuals have encountered and learn how the successful ones have plotted their journey around the hazards.

The Survival Kit

A general survival kit might be in order. The items are listed in somewhat of a priority system, but circumstances will determine which ones are most important to you.

1. Be flexible. Each of us has many talents. On some jobs you'll use one set and on another job you may use an altogether different set.
2. Be willing to take risks. Safe jobs are usually dull jobs. Chances are you'll be able to do the new job well.

3. Become as well educated as you can. Times are practically gone when you can get by without a degree. The newer, specialized, high-paying positions require at least one, and often another, advanced degree.

4. Learn as much about a new job, both in the technical area and in the people area, as you can. It's not hard to ferret out information ahead of time or at an employment interview. Remember: at the interview you want to sell yourself, but you also want to find where and with whom you'll be working, the policy on promotions, and just what the job holds for you in the future.

5. When you find that your job is dull and no longer offers challenges, start looking around. Keep your ears open. It's surprising how many good jobs there are.

6. As a general rule, don't move unless you get more money. It's just as easy to work for a good salary as it is to work for peanuts.

7. Don't leave a job too often—job-hoppers cause havoc and soon become unpopular. People begin to wonder what's wrong with you.

8. Don't knock your old company. On the other hand, don't keep reminding everybody that, "We always did it this way at XYZ."

9. Lean on other people—most people want to help you. Use your contacts to get leads about jobs, but don't be a pest. On the job, learn from both your superiors and your subordinates.

10. Take stock regularly. Do you have a plan? Are you on course? If not, what can you do about it? Changing companies is often one way of moving up, but there are other alternatives.

Blueprint for Action

Now that we have looked at a few of the dangers and only a few of the general methods of avoiding them, what is your next step? Sift out your priorities. Do you really want to search for another job or do you want to coast? How much responsibility are you willing to accept? Do you want to move your family or yourself around the country or the world in order to move upward? What do you want to do right now? Where do you want to be five, ten, twenty, or even thirty years from right now? It's important to determine your own priorities before you start to move in the management world. Being a manager means hard work, long hours, occasional loneliness, and frequent frustrations. Are you ready for it? Just as you wouldn't leave home on a long car trip without an up-to-date map, don't embark on a management career or change jobs unless you have a plan. You may have to adapt as you move, just as you might modify your itinerary while you're traveling. But if you are as well equipped as you can be, many catastrophies can be avoided.

This is my assessment of the situation today. In this book, we will explore the different steps of the long trip through the work world—explore how young, middle-aged, and senior executives look at their jobs, their careers, and their peers. Their answers to survey questions should be helpful to you as you plan your own safari through the corporate jungle.

2

The Twenties—

Finding the Path

Overview

Unlike the "flower children" of the 1960s, young people of the later 1970s and early 1980s are ambitious and success-oriented. Although there is a growing number of unemployed young people who have little education and no work experience, those included in this survey already have a firm toehold in management and are anxious to be successful by the time they are 30.

Nearly all have undergraduate degrees, which they earned with the financial support of their parents, the government, or their companies. Many are pursuing graduate degrees piecemeal, while holding down full-time jobs. The crowded night-school campuses indicate how important degrees and further education are to these young people. Again, much of the financing for graduate work comes from outside sources, especially sponsorship by a company.

More than any other age group included in the survey, people in their twenties display an earnestness and an anxiety to get a good job—one that will allow them to utilize their education. They want positions in which they will be able to use their talents, and are worried about finding the proper fit. In general, they underestimate themselves. They find it hard to critically analyze themselves, adjust their thinking, and organize their skills to make themselves as salable as possible. They lack the experience and the confidence of the older participants in the survey.

On the other hand, there is a great variety of jobs waiting for them. Those surveyed include a disc jockey, a manager of merchandise services for a local chamber of commerce, a corporate training director for a sizable chain of stores in California, an administrative resident for a large hospital in New Jersey, an assistant manager of production control in a steel plant, a compensation director responsible for 31 department stores, a research and development chemist, a senior staff accountant, an executive development coordinator, the assistant director of the New York State Department of Recreation, a senior management consultant, a vice-president of operations and personnel of a successful family-run company, a computer expert, and one who calls herself "architect, consultant, and student of the world." This wide range of jobs is a sign of the times. The ever-expanding variety of jobs should be encouraging to every young person who looks around and finds his or her own niche.

Frustrations. A fresh-faced college graduate will have to deal with many frustrations. Among them is the college recruiter, who usually has a narrow set of job specifications. Setting up interviews, making travel arrangements, and waiting in corporate lobbies can be most wearing. And rejections can be a traumatic experience.

For those chosen for jobs, the starting salaries are usually fairly high. A new recruit often makes as much as some of the old-timers on the job. Such situations are potential tinder boxes and must be handled with finesse.

After landing that first management spot, recent college graduates will usually make one job change while they're still in their twenties. This can be a rough experience because the young manager is probably unsure and afraid to lose that first job. He or she is overly anxious to be sure that the second job will be the right one.

Women in Their Twenties. Times are especially good for young women. Ten of the 25 people in this group are women. There appears little difference in the aspirations of the men and those of the women. Several of the women hold jobs once considered to be men's jobs: architect, disc jockey, chemist, executive development coordinator, hospital resident. The other five have various personnel jobs—a field where women have been traditionally welcome. Two of the women do have the top personnel spots, which, until not too long ago, was a man's province.

The women's liberation movement was mentioned by three of the women. No matter what one's opinions are about some of the tactics of the more aggressive women in the "movement," there is no doubt that they have been instrumental in making the business and management world accessible to women. As a woman who made it the hard way, before there were outside pressures to help, I am all in favor of women using their talents to the fullest extent.

How 20-Year-Olds Feel about Others. How do they feel about the older people in management? They are impatient with incompetence. They feel that some older people have rigid attitudes that cannot be influenced. They are frustrated when they can't voice their opinions or when their supervisors pay little attention to them. On the other hand, they are searching for a model or a mentor who will help move them on their way. Young managers are a strange mixture of bravado and anxiety. They want to do well and avoid mistakes, but some of their elders complain that they philosophize more than they work.

All in all, young management people are better educated, more informed, and more skilled than their older counterparts were when they were 20. As a group, they have a good start in the management field.

My Twenties

What about my own experience when I was in my twenties? They were happy years because I was young and secure in my family's love and friends' affection. Did my experiences during that time form the basis of my future work life? Hardly. It was not until I was almost 40 that I felt I was really doing a job that used my talents. I think young people now get on the right work track much earlier.

Born into a family of three boys and five girls and living on a farm in Ohio had its pleasures and its perils. My father was born in Europe and my mother was the only one in her family of 12 who was born in this country. My parents envisioned formal education, which they never had, as the key to success for their progeny. The drive for education they inspired had a profound effect on all of us. My mother was proud of the academic keys and the 30 or so diplomas she kept in a dresser drawer. This attitude is still pervasive. There are first-generation Americans in many of the night classes that I teach. They, too, know that an education is an important key.

I was in college at Bowling Green University in Ohio when the depression of the 1930s hit, and staying in school became a real problem. I worked in a restaurant at Bowling Green (where I was probably the world's worst waitress), I checked coats, and I did other odd jobs. Although tuition was shamefully low, meeting even those modest demands became a problem.

I began teaching when I was 19. It was difficult to find work, especially with only two years of college, but I was lucky. My first year as a teacher was a nightmare because I tried to follow someone else's style. Long before theories X and Y became popular in industry, there were many teachers using the old-fashioned method of paddle and pound. I, too, tried the theory X method. Fortunately for both the kids and me, I did some soul-searching and decided that there must be a better way. I learned to respect the dignity of children, learned about their talents, their strengths, and their weaknesses. It formed the basis for my work with people throughout my life. I have held that same respect for the people with whom I have dealt ever since. Young people today, too, adopt the prevailing method or technique in their field—I hope they will question it's value with more care than I did in the beginning.

Today, people assume that if they do their job well, then they can expect a boost in salary. Not so in the depression era. Eighty-eight dollars a month for eight years (each year had only nine pay periods) was the magnificent figure I was paid. My final annual salary was in the neighborhood of $1,400, a great improvement.

I was determined to finish my degree and went back to

school each summer. I finally earned my bachelor's degree in English when I was 26. After three more years of attending summer school while teaching in the winter, I received my master's.

War had broken out and many people were leaving Ohio. I was just about to turn 30, I was unhappy with my personal life, and I was restless. I decided it was time for a change. It was then I decided to go to Washington, D.C.

Did I feel sorry for myself because my education wasn't handed to me? No, but now I am impatient with young people who refuse to go to college despite their parents' pleading. All expenses paid was a luxury I never enjoyed, but I never felt shortchanged: I was always able to get what I needed. When my students at the various universities where I teach at night complain, I have some empathy, but no sympathy. Twelve years was a long time to get through college, but if I could do it, so can they.

My early work experience has given me a healthy respect for people who do menial jobs well. I know how hard it is to wait tables and to work in the field. Working with teachers and with children who were often under heavy pressures, and even lacked food, I learned compassion and acquired some of the interpersonal skills that have helped me so much over the years.

Survey Results

What about the 25 young people who answered the questionnaire? Naturally, most of them have not progressed too far up the management ladder, but many have good starts. Let's look at why they like the jobs they have.

Just as older managers do, those in their twenties enjoy jobs that give them a chance to be creative and to develop their ideas. They enjoy working with supervisors who give them credit and recognize their talents, and they appreciate the respect of their peers. They want to become experienced in their fields of expertise and want to assume responsibility. Here are a few quotes explaining what they like about their jobs:

> *Architect:* "Independence, good working conditions, respect of colleagues."
>
> *Disc Jockey:* "It is unconventional and fun—I'm involved doing things I enjoy in leisure, too, such as playing and discussing music. I enjoy the communication with many outside of my own office. My listeners communicate with me almost daily."
>
> *Recreation Director:* "I made sure that this position could give me the security I needed to finish my education and move on to bigger and better things. It does give me responsibility and practice in leadership."

The First Job. Many of those surveyed obtained their first job through the college placement office or the recruiter at their college campus. Some joined firms at which they had previously worked during the summer. Others answered ads in *The New York Times or The Wall Street Journal.* Some displayed plenty of initiative in developing resumes with good back-up material, which they put to good use. Many of them used their friends, families, or business acquaintances advantageously.

This is somewhat different from people in the older groups, who were promoted from within or used professional societies or other outside business contacts. Notice, too, the absence of the professional headhunter in finding jobs for 20-year-olds. Young people are not quite high enough in the hierarchy or in salary to be the "prey" for the executive searcher. They will be when they reach the next rung of the ladder.

Career and Personal Goals. Their career goals stretch far into the future—and why shouldn't they? A 24-year-old has 30 to 40 years of work life ahead, whereas people in their later years have perhaps less than half that amount of time. About half of the people in this group would eventually like to have their own businesses. One wants to own a retail store, another wants to be a top-flight consultant, others want to open up professional offices as architects, lawyers, or doctors. Most want eventually to have jobs where they will deal with policy determination, advanced technology, and problems on a national or international basis. If they don't already have advanced degrees, such as a master's in business administration or some other technical field, they intend to get them. Some have set up timetables, such as, "In five years I want to be associate director of my hospital, and in no more than ten years I plan to be the administrator either here or in another hospital."

The people in this age bracket in the survey put a great deal of emphasis on their personal goals as well as their professional ones. Most include a choice location in their plans, whether it be New York or a place in the Sun Belt. They opt, too, for family life and are more apt to follow the traditional paths than those who graduated in the 1960s. Their plans include other members of their family whom they want to see happy. This can be a hazard as far as an individual job is concerned, but most think they can manage both job and home well. This is in contrast to the men and women in their late thirties, forties, and older. To these executives, the job comes first and the family is supposed to adjust to the changes. Here are a few quotes from those in their twenties:

> "I feel professional goals need to be kept in perspective. To me, personal happiness and fulfillment are most important. These can be achieved partially through meeting professional goals."

> "My professional goals are very much related to my belief that separation of work and life is a sick notion."

> "My personal goals involve finding an aesthetic and healthy, loving environment in the country. I must become at least comfortably wealthy. This is where my wish to study law comes in. I have already achieved the goal of a satisfying love relationship. This has caused some slight loss of flexibility in my career (location). I am not very job-oriented; I am more interested in travel and other personal pleasures made possible from a job I like."

Are these goals realistic? As the budding architect says, "There hasn't been a hitch yet." Or, as another puts it, "Certainly these are dreams, but I feel my potential and achievements have been recognized and utilized and will be in the future." Still another says, "I think I can do whatever I set out to do. I'm really motivated and I expect to reach the goals I have set."

There are always a few who just can't seem to get started right. They leave their first job after a month or so because the firm's needs and the applicants' talents are not properly matched, or because the 20-year-old expected too much from his or her first job. Many took their first job just to get started and don't plan to stay there very long. Here is how they answer the question: "How long do you plan to stay on your job?"

> "Several more months."

"Another four to six months."
"Two years."
"Four to 12 months."
"One more year."
"Promotion pending."
"My range is four to five years in this position."
"Two to three years."
"One year."

Average it all out and it amounts to about one year. There are several people in their later twenties who have recently moved to their second position, and one has had two previous jobs.

I'd say that their goals are great: they want families, good jobs, and time to enjoy life. Because they are talented, ambitious, and well educated, they should be able to achieve their professional goals. One can hope, in spite of the high divorce rates of young people, that they will meet their cherished personal goals for a happy family life.

Complaints about Jobs. People in this group do have complaints about their current jobs. They had expected more professionalism on the job than they have encountered. Some have to make too many decisions when they are still unsure of themselves. Some are unhappy because of their boss's attitude. "I would like to see the boss do some of the follow-up work. Image of the boss spouting ideas and leaving the scene is irritating," says one. Most complaints center around lack of growth, unclear promotion paths, and lack of challenge. Many in the survey group see no further development possible and are updating their resumes. For example, a chemist said he doesn't use his knowledge of chemistry on his present job and hopes to find a position where he will. An expert typist with an economics degree can't get loose from her typewriter in her current job. She, too, wants to move elsewhere.

Even though there are risks involved, these young people would rather take that chance than stay where they are. What are the reasons given for changing jobs?

"After much internal searching, I discovered that my career goals were not being met. My biggest goal is to have control over my own time and the opportunity to express my creativity. I wanted to find a position where I could express these needs in an organization that complemented them."

"I was sure my future wasn't selling life insurance. I firmly believe the most important thing about a career (job) is that you totally enjoy what you are doing. I am also sure that my current position isn't long term, not because of the nature of the job, but because I don't enjoy it enough to do it for the rest of my life."

"I wanted to leave operations and get back to working with people."

They have named most of the reasons anyone would change jobs—more money, more responsibility, more appreciation, and a faster promotion track. Most young people with whom I converse and whom my executive friends tell me about are impatient and want promotions faster than management can produce them. "In fact," says one friend, who is president of a company, "an applicant in his twenties told me he wanted my job in ten years. It took me 40 to get it. I hired him because I was willing to take a chance. If he doesn't leave me, he may make it in 15 years or so."

You can see the confidence of these young people as they face the future. They seem, too, to have great financial security.

However, in contrast to people in the older age groups, who have learned restraint, the young people surveyed became impatient if their talents aren't recognized quickly enough. Repetitive work and boring jobs are not for them. It takes a while before they recognize that what's promised in the books or at the recruiter's desk is different from the day-to-day operations of a company, hospital, or any other business. It also takes a while to discover that almost every job has a routine aspect that must be endured. Even presidents must read boring reports and listen to outlandish proposals. It takes some seasoning before the person in his or her twenties learns the interpersonal skills necessary to do the job.

Turning Points. There seem to be specific times or circumstances that cause people in their twenties to take a different direction. Some changes are planned, some come about by chance, and some result from personal circumstances. These same abrupt changes also occur when people are in their thirties and perhaps their forties. However, for those in their fifties and sixties, some changes occur abruptly as a result of circumstances out of one's control, such as mergers, failures of companies, or even firings. For people in their twenties, changing paths is a more planned procedure than for most older people. There are exceptions to this general rule, as you will see in later chapters. Here are a few of the turning points identified by the young people in this age group:

> "Purchase of a home, marriage, availability of capital for investment."

> "The turning point in my career was joining a multi-million-dollar company and discovering that I got fewer personal rewards by working within a highly structured development."

"My marriage. It meant responsibility not only for myself, but for dependents."

"College graduation, plus a supervisor who was willing to develop subordinates."

"My parents' divorce when I was 20. My tour of duty for two years as a medic in the Air Force. Facing the job market without a master's degree."

Hazards.   The hazards of the twenties include facing the stiff competition for good jobs, choosing an unsatisfactory first job, and encountering difficulty in finding the next job. Employers are looking for experienced people and are often unwilling to take a chance on the young, untried job hunter.

Dealing with office politics can be hazardous. Beware of taking sides in a political situation; you may be kicked out with the "culprit." (This is more apt to happen if you are close to the top and are forced to take sides.) Those surveyed identified the following hazards:

"Over-criticism of my colleagues. Dirty fighting for position—the old battle of protecting one's turf."

"Many of us find the boss is inaccessible in a crisis. Then when a calamity happens he asks why notification wasn't given at the proper time."

"I have confided in too many people. I will have to be more reserved and learn whom to talk to."

Do's and Don'ts.   Closely tied to the hazards are the lists of undesirable behaviors and attitudes that those in their twenties have prepared. Traits to be shunned include failing to follow up, trying to do everything by one's self, forgetting to ask for help, becoming a yes-man, spreading oneself too thin, not following directions, and faking the job.

It is important not to assume that others are inept. This seems like such a well-accepted fact that perhaps it shouldn't be mentioned, but to me it is essential to assume that people are competent and have many talents until that assumption is proved otherwise. When I hear, "I have the dumbest subordinate in the world," or "My boss is so stupid, I just can't see how he possibly holds his position," or similar remarks, I am suspicious of the "genius" who is blowing off. In addition, avoid talking behind someone's back, cutting corners, and just plain goofing off.

On the other side of the coin are the wonderful "green signals" for the young. Most of them are full of hope and enthusiasm. They have not had time for disillusionment. A new plant opens and needs people with special skills— the young person has all the newest technological training. A knowledgeable boss or supervisor recognizes a comer and recommends him or her for a promotion.

As stated in the beginning of the chapter, there are thousands of new jobs every year and young people are geared to meet them. Schools (in spite of the criticism leveled against them) are turning out graduates who can make the transition from academia to the work world without too much trauma. It's a bright world, barring catastrophe, for the young of today. They are smart, well informed, and sure of themselves. At least that's the way the ones included in the survey look.

Just as they have lists of no-no's for their current jobs, they also know what they should do to add to their chances of success. Here is one composite list of do's:

1. Know what you want.
2. Know your job thoroughly.
3. Grasp the whole organizational structure.

4. Let employees know who is in charge.
5. Don't overplay your role.
6. Know the needs of employees.
7. Gain and give recognition for a job well done.
8. Give your subordinates and your boss your support.
9. Be consistent in judgments.
10. Be fair.
11. Be willing to do your share of the dirty work.
12. Communicate—establish feedback.
13. Have vision.
14. Have goals.
15. Do careful work.
16. Have concepts of cost.
17. Meet deadlines.
18. Be stylish.
19. Be polite, be conscientious, and work hard.

Grasping the whole structure helps keep your job in perspective. Even in large companies it is important to know where you fit in, what your role is. If you become so involved in one little section or project, you are bound to feel either lost or overimportant. Both you and your subordinates need to know what the finished product is and what role you play in making the company successful.

When you are young, it is difficult to make sure everyone knows you are boss without being obnoxious. This is especially true if your subordinates are older than you are. Lack of respect for the leader is one sure sign of failure in a department, division, or company.

Doing your share of the dirty work shows your subordinates that you appreciate the work that some of them do all the time. The boss who will move cartons, stuff envelopes, occasionally arrange for his or her own airplane tickets, or get coffee helps win over the group.

However, don't carry this to an extreme—your time must be put to its best use.

Meet deadlines. If you learn that lesson early in the game then you have a chance to move into upper management. It is still a shock to me that this important rule is not stressed in management training. Program Evaluation and Review Technique (PERT) can help you understand where your project fits into the larger scheme; you may then be less likely to undermine a project's effectiveness by missing deadlines. Failing to meet deadlines can hold you back from a promotion, so if you can see that you won't be able to meet a deadline, let management know about it well in advance.

The respondents had these general comments to offer on the topic of do's and don'ts:

"I believe the strongest do is to believe in yourself, because if you don't no one else will either."

"Never give up and show perseverance if you want to succeed."

"I believe communication should be practiced as a two-way affair—both up and down. Today people are sometimes afraid to talk to each other. . . . Employees should be encouraged by supervisors to communicate. If managers are not aware of 'what's happening,' problems do arise."

"A good manager should try to balance his attempt to follow the organization's objectives with an appreciation for those of his subordinates. These two aspects are important to his success."

These comments express the desire of young people to blend work and outside living, to reconcile personal and work goals, and to utilize their talents. They differ from the older participants in that they show more awareness of others, while still having driving ambitions to get things done *and* enjoy the good life.

Conclusion: As we have seen in the examples cited above, the work world offers plenty of challenges. And no matter how exotic or strange many jobs may seem, there are young people who are qualified to fill those openings. Their capabilities and enthusiasm are boundless, and soon they'll be running the world of work with expertise and finesse.

Case Study: Allison Rogers, Architect

Allison is an only child of parents who were in their early forties when she was born. She had the economic advantages that might not have been possible if she had been born when they were in their twenties. However, both parents worked in executive positions, so Allison spent many lonely moments as a child. During her childhood, she endured a series of housekeepers, but fortunately for her each one was impressed by the friendliness and the charm of the youngster. The housekeepers ranged from an embittered divorcee to a young woman entranced with fairy tales and simple pleasures. (The variety of people helped the child learn tolerance and understanding.)

Her parents decided to send their daughter to the best private schools in the city. Her education included four years at Princeton where she obtained a degree in architecture. After working a year in an architect's office in the West, she returned to school and obtained her master's from the University of Southern California. Her work experience includes architectural work for the government and private industry, and related experience at a university.

Married and living in Austria, she recognizes the difficulties of entering the workforce in a foreign country, but a semi-mastery of the language is helping her overcome those barriers. She now works full time for an architecture firm and spends her spare time teaching English to Austrians and people from other countries.

What does she see as the problems of the young professional? If you're bright, there are many paths that look intriguing. The question is which to choose. Because you must decide early in life which direction to take, you are apt to question later on whether or not you made the right decision. By then, however, school and professional studies have already set the mold.

She feels, however, that you must establish professional credibility in at least one field even though there might be some questions about having made an early choice. This means getting professional accreditation and experience. After these are obtained, she feels there is still time to branch out.

She hopes to do large-scale projects and finally, when she gains expertise, to act as a consultant to governments or big engineering firms. She states that being too set on long-range goals might make a person so one-sided that it would be impossible to stay flexible enough to take advantage of exciting projects that might come along.

She hopes to go into private practice with her husband, who is an architect, and to eventually establish an international firm. She recognizes that a two-career marriage can create some problems. But, like so many other young women, she does not see her professional career as a hindrance to raising a family and having a happy household.

She has always enjoyed the people with whom she has worked. All of her employers seemed sorry to see her go and told her she would always be welcomed back. So she, like some of the other smart young people included in the study, looks forward to both a satisfying family and a satisfying work life. Her ideals and standards are high, and with any kind of break she should succeed.

3

The Thirties—

The Searching Years

Overview

Working people in their thirties are on the move more than people in any other age group. Capable managers know that good jobs abound, and those in this group are determined to find the positions that will act as springboards to successful careers. We often see people making two or three job changes during this ten-year period. That means they're taking risks, because no matter how bad a current job looks, the new one may involve so many unknowns that it is hard to adjust to. People in their thirties can afford to take such risks partly because most of them are free from the excessive financial responsibilities that executives in their forties must deal with. But they are more careful about job changes now than they were in their twenties.

They are, however, willing to leave their old jobs if they become disenchanted with their progress and find that they cannot become the top executive fast enough. Most think they have the capabilities of being the chief executive officer, or close to it. They have not yet become disillusioned with their own capabilities, as often happens to those who are over 50 and still haven't "made it." Older people are more apt to recognize their limitations or circumstances and don't push as hard to move to the top.

Characteristically, a person in his or her thirties will thoroughly investigate a new job possibility. Is the company listed in *Standard & Poor's Register?* What is its reputation in the industry? Will the new job offer enough money to warrant changing? Often, a move entails several interviews before the candidate and the management of the new firm are satisfied that it will be advantageous for both. A potential job-changer checks with friends, current employees, and anyone else who might have pertinent information or advice, in order to be as sure as possible that the right move is being made. A quote from one executive in the survey is representative of his age group's attitude toward change:

> "I was getting bored with being Number Two man when my boss was only 51 years old. When the opportunity came to be Number One in a large firm, I investigated all the angles. I found that the firm was solid, had progressive policies, and offered me a much higher salary. I accepted and find that the added responsibilities and decision making as a vice-president are just what I needed. My work world is great and I am pleased that I had enough sense to leave the old scene for the new. My children are growing—I'll eventually have three in college at the same time, so the extra income also helps."

The thirties are also characterized by shifts in direction. There is a reevaluation of goals, of position, of family, and of opportunity. During these years, many people complete their night-school education. Encouragement received from a supervisor, drastic personal or family changes (such as divorce or the death of a loved one), and chance meetings with old bosses, headhunters, or peers at technical conventions add to the fast movement of people in this age group.

Most people in their thirties obtain interesting and high-paying jobs. In fact, at the end of this decade of their lives they sometimes receive two to three times as much as they did when in their twenties. Here are some of the jobs held by these ambitious men and women: vice-president of personnel; benefits administrator for a billion-dollar company; vice-president of marketing for a computer firm; director of long-range planning; administrator of a 300-bed hospital; corporate director of management development; assessment-center manager; and plant superintendant of a major automobile plant. These executives are not taking unnecessary chances, nor are they shirking their current jobs. They are digging in for the long haul. They are old enough to have forgotten some of the frivolities of their twenties and are set on having a good job with commensurate pay.

Women in Their Thirties   More women are represented in this age category than in any other group in the survey. Almost one-fourth are women, whereas in the older age breaks they were a rarity (for example, only one-tenth are women in the 40-to-50 age group). True, our sample is small, but this does follow the general pattern of more detailed and lengthy studies.

Families are important to both men and women. Most have children in grade school or high school and are somewhat reluctant to take a job which would entail moving them from their current surroundings. This doesn't seem to deter too many, however. Dual career marriages are cropping up more and more frequently.

This may be a problem of the future, especially for women now in their twenties who are obtaining jobs comparable to their male counterparts.

My Thirties

When I was between 30 and 40, I was searching for a spot where I could operate without getting into a rut. It was a time of chance-taking. I cannot say, as some do, that I carefully planned each move I made during this period. I knew I was unhappy where I was, but had no clear-cut idea of where I belonged. In looking back I see that it was a time of drastic personal adjustment in which I learned much about working in areas other than teaching.

I had finished the long, hard, 12-year grind of getting my master's degree, but found that I was teaching the same way I had always been teaching, with only a change of the faces in front of me. I was unmarried and yearning for personal security. Just as everyone else was during that period, I was restless and unhappy because I wasn't directly involved in the war effort.

On my thirtieth birthday, after an unhappy love affair which added even more to my restlessness, I took the advice of my brother and decided to try working in Washington, D.C., for the summer. With my teaching contract for the next year tucked firmly in my pocket, I departed for Washington; I never really went home again.

I found the atmosphere in Washington heady and exciting. After a few weeks I found a job selling children's books at Woodward and Lothrop's. Even though I thought that job might develop into a great career, the pay was below what my teaching salary had been and was considerably less than low-ranking professional jobs in the government. It seemed that almost everyone was looking for a government job, so I was lucky to find one with the Bureau of Labor Statistics of the U.S. Department of Labor. During the war years, government jobs were on a temporary basis, so I was taking a chance by leaving the security of Woodward and Lothrop's.

With little training, but with some skills in mathematics and statistics, I became a wage analyst for the Bureau of Labor Statistics. The job consisted in tabulating wage information on what are now ancient calculating machines. Wage surveys, so common in industry today, were just emerging then. There was little comparative wage data for any industry. The BLS furnished data used by the burgeoning War Labor Board to decide who would get wage increases.

I was asked to help set up the New York office of the Bureau. As a field agent, I collected wage information from industries throughout New York and New Jersey. Field agents had always been men, and the horror with which some of those agents greeted me—a woman— should not be hard to imagine. However, those men overcame their initial shock and proceeded to teach me as much as they knew.

Thus began a most interesting career. Airplane factories in Buffalo, canning factories in Lockport, wineries in the Finger Lakes region, and law offices and restaurants in New York are just a few of the industries we gathered wage data from. During my five years at the BLS I visited several hundred plants and company headquarters. Before I left the BLS, I became a supervisor of 20 or so agents, wrote final reports, and made presentations to the War Labor Board.

After the war, the inevitable cutting back of federal

employees hit the BLS hard. Even though I was assured that I would be retained in some capacity, I decided it was time to look elsewhere.

What did I gain from my sojourn at the BLS? A healthy and lasting respect for what industry can accomplish. I found I had the courage to tackle new challenges. I learned to supervise and found out who were slouches and who were strivers. I learned how to write reports and to present conclusions. My experience there formed the foundation for much of my future work.

Do other people in their thirties learn as much from their jobs as I did then, or did the war years push us so much harder that, of necessity, we tried the untried and produced the almost impossible? It is hard to tell, but my own experience was as fulfilling as it could be under the strain of wartime, when almost everyone has at least one relative involved in extreme danger.

My next job was with the National Foremen's Institute, where I wrote about wages in a weekly report. I explored union contracts for stories, visited companies in search of exciting employee relations practices, and collaborated with other reporters in the same field.

By the end of my thirties, I began to think about arranging for a "safe" future. I expect that people who weathered the Depression of the 1930s never feel entirely financially secure. We worry about security much more than do the younger people of today. Labor relations reporting just didn't seem to furnish that security. It was flashy and satisfying, but I thought I needed an established firm that would provide stability. I didn't know myself very well at that time; my judgment was wrong. I flourish best when there is a certain degree of uncertainty and when I can run my own show. So it was again with reluctance that I began to think about another position. Fortunately or unfortunately, that is why I switched to a research organization—the one spot which proved a treacherous hole instead of a safe upward road.

Tremendous changes in my personal life—a divorce, a second marriage, and the purchase of a home—helped make my thirties an exciting time.

Were my thirties different from those of the people who answered the survey? The chief difference, I believe, is that the survey respondents seem to calculate their changes much more carefully. There may be some who made changes the way I did—as a result of outside pressures or fortuitous circumstances—but most of them seem more highly qualified for their new jobs than I was and build on their education and knowledge better than I did. They may have had an easier time in becoming qualified: few have had to deal with major interruptions in their career paths. They plan their course with the same attention to detail that they focus on the major work projects.

Survey Results

Twenty-four executives in their thirties participated in the survey. Their jobs included those mentioned earlier in this chapter. Many had achieved vice-presidential status or were heads of major departments in large companies. They were already beginning to carry heavy responsibilities, especially those in their later thirties.

What are these people really like? What are the "green signals" in their current jobs that point the way to bigger and better opportunities? They like the chance to be creative, to utilize their talents, to influence corporate direction, and to work with other highly motivated people. They enjoy problem-solving and want to use their own initiative. One person likes being a big fish in a little pond and another enjoys being involved in community affairs. Practically all illustrate the fact that under the right circumstances, work can be enjoyable as well as lucrative. However, there are obstacles. People in their thirties are becoming more and more aware that the business world has its danger spots. In this competitive world of work, one must keep alert in order to survive.

In this age group, lack of support, misunderstanding, and lack of direction are the main causes for job dissatisfaction. Note that these are factors that keep people from moving up. Some of those surveyed do not respect the top managers, and criticize them for failing to delegate properly, which creates an unhappy work situation. Poor communication, lack of staff, intervention of the government, company politics, and interpersonal problems are some of the other hazards. Making the wrong decision about accepting a new job and staying in one job too long (11 years in one case) are also mentioned.

Many of the 30-year-olds complain about the difficulty of selling an idea to top management. For those of us who believe that selling to top management is 75 percent of the battle, this complaint rings true. The restless person in his thirties is looking for a situation in which new ideas are encouraged and backed by management.

Need for Support. Support is a key word that was mentioned frequently by people in this age group. They have moved far enough up the ladder so they are not as dependent on others as they were in their twenties, but they have not yet reached a position of complete independence. They know the importance of support from below, and most of them have learned, sometimes the hard way, that they must earn this support. But their chief concern seems to be with securing support from top management—the place where decisions about their careers are made.

Here is how a few of those surveyed describe their situation:

> "Chairman of the Board, formerly a personnel officer, has feeling for the area and is very supportive."

> "CEO very supportive, as is the president. They have high standards, but are willing to take the time to teach."

> "They are supportive, but spend too little time understanding the nature of what I do."

> "Available for counsel, but not oppressive. Will provide necessary dollars to support sensible programs."

> "I report to the president, who respects my field and myself."

> "I am very much involved in the management of the company. My function is highly regarded. My input is always asked."

Reasons for Changing Jobs. Even though many are pleased with their current jobs, most would move—and many do. When asked whether they would change jobs, some hedged their answers—they are looking for an ideal spot. Here is how some of them completed the statement, "I would change jobs if _____."

> "I didn't like my boss; if my opinions were not asked; if I didn't respect the company or the management."

> "I could find an organization similar to the one I am with in terms of growth and success. If I could have a direct

reporting relationship to the chief executive. If I could find a chief executive with high moral/ethical standards in dealing with people."

"Another opportunity arose with the same advantages I have now, but located in the Northeast."

"I were sure something else would be more interesting or stimulating."

Career and Personal Goals. What about their career goals? Practically all said they had career goals and had worked out specific strategies for achieving those goals. Executives in their thirties want much out of life. They recognize the importance of family and personal fulfillment in addition to success on the job. In this respect they aren't so different from people in other groups, but they are more aware that the thirties are the critical years for changing jobs. How do they describe their long- and short-term goals?

"Perform well enough to become president either of this company or of another."

"If I may sound corny, to practice the Golden Rule."

"To be the best there is in the field."

"My personal goals are to be independent and free to make choices. I'd like to be successful, well paid, and fulfilled in my professional goals. Personal and professional goals must interact continually. The two seem to interact much more at this time than they did in my earlier business years. Earlier, business came first and outside interests, personal development, even marriage and family had to fit around the all-important devotion to success on the job. I have reevaluated the priorities and feel the balance is better now, and was wrong in my earlier years."

"Personally and professionally I want growth, stimulation, challenge, and fullness."

Factors Influencing Success. What factors helped people in this group become successful? Table 1 shows how respondents assess the importance of certain items to their careers. (Numbers indicate percent of respondents who checked that answer.)

Table 1. Importance of selected factors
on success of people in their thirties.

	Very Important	Important	Unimportant
Education	80%	10%	10%
Upbringing and Friends	25%	75%	
Marriage and Family	45%	45%	1%
Mentors or Role Models	50%	50%	
Supervisors or Superiors	40%	40%	10%
Personal Interests	50%	50%	
Mergers and Acquisitions		20%	80%

Note the importance of education. The respondents who rate it as unimportant are not college graduates. They have made it to their current positions without a degree. But it is getting harder to find a young person at an upper-management position who doesn't have a degree or who doesn't indicate education as one of the important factors in his or her growth. Note, too, the emphasis on mentors or role models. All respondents rate this factor as important or very important. Marriage and family also receive high marks, even though the rate of divorce is fairly high in this age group.

The breakdown of statements pertaining to their

Table 2. Statements about work in the thirties.

	Agree Strongly	Agree	Disagree	Disagree Strongly
Job success is important to my self-image.	60%	40%		
Personal accomplishments off the job are the most important source of an individual's self-image.		45%	45%	5%
Long-term career planning is difficult to achieve.		5%	45%	5%
Most people's career plans are more dreams than strategies.		70%	20%	10%
Career advancement is often as much luck as strategy.	5%	40%	60%	
Job satisfaction is more important than job advancement.	5%	45%	45%	
Who you know is more important than what you do.			90%	10%
It's better to switch employers to gain more opportunity than to await promotion from within.	10%	40%	40%	10%
Slow but steady advancement will get you further than job-hopping.	5%	30%	60%	5%
Family or personal commitments should come before ambition.	5%	50%	45%	
Most people have made it into the line of advancement by age 35.		50%	40%	10%

Table 2. Continued.

	Agree Strongly	Agree	Disagree	Disagree Strongly
If you haven't made the grade by age 40, you'll never make it.		30%	60%	10%
Most people over 55 are more concerned with retirement than with career advance-ment.		50%	50%	
Immediate superiors are the most impor-tant influences on one's advancement.		85%	15%	
A spouse can make or break a career.		50%	50%	
Job security is more important than job advancement.			90%	10%
After one gets to be 40 or so, it is better to stay with one firm than to switch employers.		40%	60%	

careers is shown in Table 2. All respondents agree that job success is important to one's self-image, again confirming the impact of work on one's personal life. Although recognizing its importance, many believe that long-term planning is difficult to achieve and that often career planning is more a dream than a strategic action. No one surveyed thinks that job security is more important than job advancement. Yet they split on whether a person should job-hop or make steady advancement. Half feel that a spouse can make or break a career—a higher percentage than in the older age groups. They all agree that what you do is more important than whom you know, and almost all concur that immediate supervisors have much to do with one's career advancement.

Holding a Job: Do's and Don'ts. When asked about the most important things to do to keep a management position, this group's answers are similar to those of the older age groups. Here are some of their responses:

Do's
1. Make significant contributions and get results.
2. Understand the informal structure and build relationships.
3. Select good subordinates.
4. Give controlled latitude to subordinates.
5. Be aware of the job above yours and be prepared to fill it at any time. Keep two steps ahead of the duties of your job description. Understand the person next below you and train him or her to fill your shoes.
6. Keep physically fit.
7. Keep current with change.
8. Have a sense of humor.

Don'ts
1. Don't be lazy.
2. Don't be dishonest.
3. Don't be indecisive.
4. Don't be timid.
5. Don't miss deadlines.
6. Don't get fat.
7. Don't ignore the informal organization.
8. Don't let status be most important.
9. Don't be nice at the cost of being effective.
10. Don't be concerned about getting all the credit.
11. Don't be afraid to make decisions or to express your opinions.

Note that energy and health are mentioned several times. Even though hard physical work is seldom required of executives, the increasing pressures and demands on time require good health and stamina. Today, executives require a high energy level in order to get things done.

When asked about the biggest mistakes in career planning in management, the answers were revealing:

"If I had it to do over again, I would have completed my doctorate at an earlier age. I would have selected a more prestigious university. I would have taken more risks in entrepreneurial ventures."

"I was moved up too quickly; I should have had more experience in lower-level jobs."

"Selling my ideas."

"Too much insensitivity to peer groups."

"Getting embroiled in company politics. I was lucky to come out of it unscathed."

"Not striving to develop relationships with key people when they opened the door for me to do so."

"Trying to do too many things at once. Diluting efforts."

Conclusion. Even though they like their current jobs, men and women in their thirties are not wed to them. They would change for more money, an opportunity to go back to Maine or elsewhere with the same opportunities and more money, or for more responsibilities and challenges. People in their thirties are a restless lot, and even when everything is fine on the current job, they are still looking for an even more ideal spot.

In summary, people in their thirties are really on the move. The strong replies from both men and women about their careers, their goals, and how they believe management should work indicate that they have a high opinion of themselves, their work, and their management. There were few complaints. Their reaction was positive and their plans for action affirmative.

Case Study: Eugene Masters, Chief Engineer of a Large Corporation in New York

Eugene is in his early thirties, is married to an intelligent wife, and has two small children. He typifies the young executive on the move who is happy with both his work and his home situation.

He is enthusiastic about his job. He supervises six other people, many of whom know little English. His strengths lie in his enthusiasm, his knowledge of his job, and his ability to communicate well with both subordinates and executives who bring their problems of heat, ventilation, or air conditioning to him.

Like others in their thirties, he likes his freedom in making decisions—an important factor for everyone included in their study.

He was recently promoted to his present position when his boss retired. Management evidently has faith in him: They are paying for his college courses at night and are sending him to seminars at universities and management centers.

Eugene's company is expanding and moving from an old facility to a new one, so he is optimistic about his job in the foreseeable future. Unlike some young executives, he feels that because of the company's investment in him, he owes them some allegiance.

He spent four years in the Army in Southeast Asia.

Like many other servicemen, he realizes that an education will help him attain goals he had never considered pursuing when he left home. He attends night school and is working toward an MBA. He leads a well-rounded life that includes fishing, camping, golf, and tennis, so the future should indeed be a bright one.

Born into a family of nine with a restless father and a mother who was a nurse, he lived in England for a year and made many trips to the Bahamas. He looks forward to pleasure in seeing his children grow and to enjoying trips with his wife.

How many young people are there like Eugene? Plenty, if those included in the study are a sample of a much larger segment of young American executives on the move.

Case Study: Joseph Green, Vice-President of a Major Bank

The American dream of success has been a reality to Joe Green. However, his link to the holocaust in Europe still haunts him. He remembers back to when he was 4 years old in his native country of Lithuania. The Germans rounded up crowds of women and children, who were taken away and shot. His father, who was determined that his family would survive, worked as a mechanic on the tanks of the Germans. Hiding in deep cellars became a way of life. Joseph's father exchanged all his worldly goods with a farmer to secure safety for his son. Joseph still remembers the shot of liquor he was given to quiet him down as he was carted off in a potato sack to the farmer's home. Jospeh's mother, unfortunately, did not survive. The older Green married his sister-in-law and escaped across the East-West border with a tired little boy. The family spent four years in West Germany. Then a group in the Bronx raised enough money to sponsor the Green family in America.

Life in America was not easy. Mr. Green became a chicken plucker and his wife cleaned bed pans at a local hospital. Not an auspicious beginning, but the advantages of a free education in the good schools of New York provided a ray of hope. Joseph was picked to go to one of the top high schools in Manhattan. However, the young scholar was disappointed because his family worried about his trip on the subways alone, so he went to the closest high school in the Bronx. Joseph wonders how different his life might have been if he had attended the technical/engineering high school.

Joseph took odd jobs to get through school. He waited tables, ran errands, and acted as a guard to earn extra cash. He applied the same kind of persistence to obtaining a master's degree, and it paid off. He was recruited at City College 14 years ago by a major New York bank.

Prior to that, he had worked for the New York State Employment Service, first as an interviewer and then as an examiner who determined whether or not an applicant was eligible for unemployment benefits. That job exposed him to a "slice of life" that helped him in making decisions about people. He became adept at separating the real from the faker, the deserving from the undeserving.

Hired as a trainee, his game plan included becoming a vice-president within ten years. He became vice-president of personnel in nine and a half years. He now supervises a variety of bank operations, including restaurants with budgets of millions of dollars. He is ambitious, and wants to become a senior vice-president, so he will have more of a voice in policy-making.

He attributes his success to planning, to hard work, and

to an open-management style (he puts heavy emphasis on team management). He is concerned about those he supervises and is especially aware of talents that might be passed over by other people. For example, he recently promoted a secretary to a personnel spot, and he will now carefully watch the progress of that person. His faults, he thinks, lie in being too direct, and being too impatient with incompetence.

He is a realist about what he calls the Machiavellian nature of corporate politics and, possibly because of his early tragedies, believes that any person has the potential to do almost anything to another human being. So in his makeup are great gentleness and faith combined with an awareness of how brutal life can be, both in and out of the corporate world.

As a good manager, he lobbies to get facts before making decisions, has learned to ask vital and particular questions to clear away confusion, and knows the importance of surrounding himself with people he can trust. He knows that you can't be successful in a vacuum, that you must have ideas and someone near at hand whom you can bounce them against. He is representative of managers in their thirties who are well on the way to success and are eager to continue moving up.

4

The Forties—

The Restless Years

Overview

Today, the majority of people in their forties are restless and looking for an opportunity to move up. They are afraid if they don't make advantageous changes now, there will be fewer and fewer opportunities to do so later. They are usually somewhat more conservative than they were in their twenties and thirties, and will examine each new job offer with great care. Job-hopping has been replaced by a more somber approach to career planning. However, executives in their forties are more restless than those in their fifties or sixties. They are looking for positions with more money and more responsibility than their current jobs offer. Family financial demands contribute to the pressure: those who are parents are anxious that their children earn college degrees. (Anyone who has looked at college costs knows what a financial strain they can be.)

The management world is still a tight circle. People in their forties rely on their reputations, qualifications, and contacts when changing jobs. Most feel they can no longer change as frequently as they did before. If someone has moved six or seven times by the time he is in his mid-forties, and is looking to move again, potential employers will probably look askance at such a record. They will wonder whether a job-hopper is worth the investment of time and money—he may stay only a short time.

In contrast to such mobile executives, there are still a substantial number who believe that their age makes it impossible for them to move. Some lack a formal education or are afraid to lose their financial security. As one respondent put it, "If I had had the opportunity to complete all my education in my early twenties, I would have shopped around and worked for different companies, instead of staying with the same company, which is what I did. . . . Now, after working for one company for over 20 years in a specialty field, I'm afraid to move."

People in this group give plenty of credit to being at the right place at the right time. They disagree strongly with the notion that who you know is more important than what you do. They think you should be pretty well in the line of advancement by age 35, but feel that you can still make it after 40. In spite of their concern for money and prestige, job security is not the most important thing in life, as it is later on.

The forties are a time of soul-searching and reevaluation. People ask themselves, "Is this what I want to do the rest of my life?" "Can I move anywhere else in this job and in this company?" "Is this company sound and will I have a secure spot for the foreseeable future?" "Where else can I go?"

My Forties

My own forties were a mixture of rough times and recovery, excitement and turmoil. I had left my job at the

National Foremen's Institute for one with an old-line management research organization, which I thought would be safer. I hesitate to use the name because it was the one time in my life when I was really unhappy with my work. I went there with high hopes, intending to stay for the rest of my life. Unfortunately, I found the atmosphere there stuffy—the jobs and the functions were compartmentalized, so that there was little chance for me to break down barriers. In addition, for the first time in my career I found someone who resented me and who fought me every step of the way. This is one of the hazards of changing jobs at any age. You must find out who your friends are in a new job and must learn whether you are inadvertently taking over someone else's duties. Some older employees are strong enough to wreck your chances of success if they feel their territory has been invaded. In my case, the "witch" bided her time and was at least partially responsible for my next change of job.

Still, the job had its advantages. It was the only nine-to-five job I've ever had and I brought no job-related problems home with me—which was convenient, because that was a hectic, exciting period of my personal life. My husband and I bought a house and, at the age of 41, I became a mother. For the first time in my life, I found it difficult to keep my home affairs in order while working.

At the end of two years, I came back from a short vacation and found that my boss had been fired—and a new man was waiting to break some bad news to me about my own status. I shall never forget that scene nor my terrible feelings of inadequacy. I had done a good job and have always believed that I was released for no good reason, partially through the efforts of the displeased person who had influence with the top. Within a week I had four offers of positions much better than the one I was leaving behind, but the shock of that interview still haunts me.

What did I learn from this experience? First, job security is never guaranteed. Second, there are unscrupulous climbers who would like to use your cracked skull to boost themselves up the ladder, and unless you are alert, they'll be successful. Third, good friends in business who know your work record can be helpful when you need them. Fourth, don't be beaten by disaster. I have seen both sides of the coin. Those who recover from the first rough shock go on to bigger and better jobs, and are wiser than they were before. But those who wallow in self-pity and give up are seldom seen on management row again. It takes courage and guts to survive.

Some people are surprised to find that executives are often fired quite unceremoniously. "You're fired!" "I quit!" These loud statements can still be heard in management halls. Usually, however, the dagger is held with a velvet glove. If you are ever asked to leave a job, remember that the time you spend at the old job once the ax has fallen will be a time of trauma. You'll suddenly become a pariah. Only a few good friends will stick by you.

In my case, everything happened at once. A new baby, a mortgage, high family expenses—and no job! However, through my old boss in the firm that I had left, I heard about the opening for an assistant in the personnel division of American Management Associations. Without any lapse in work time I began to work at AMA, which had just started its seminar program. Before I left AMA some six years later, we were putting together 300 seminars a year and were running several courses and major meetings. My job was to get the speakers, help outline the subject matter, and then see that everything was run up to high AMA standards. This meant travel to

Chicago, to Dallas, to Washington, D.C., and to many other cities.

In those days, AMA was a great jumping off place for young men with talent. In my six years there, I had five immediate bosses. (That was before women were as assertive as they are now.) Between home and work, I had about all the responsibility I could handle. As a result, I did not object when one person after another moved into the top divisional spot. It gave me the peculiar advantages of often knowing more about the division than the rolling stones who were my bosses. I enjoyed working in an atmosphere that gave me room to use my own ideas.

From my experience at AMA, I learned many things, including: how to be flexible enough to adjust to different leadership styles; how to take advantage of the knowledge available from industry executives (many of whom have remained friends over the years); what the advantages of a staunch support staff are; how to manage home and office, even when there are children; what the beautiful results of team effort can be; and how to budget so that income more than matches outgo.

Why did I leave AMA? A boost in salary of $5,000, a vice-presidency, and a chance to work with the same boss who had hired me at AMA were the lures that brought me to my next job, vice-president of the American Association of Industrial Management (AAIM). Like other people in their forties, I was willing to leave a secure spot and take a calculated risk to receive more money and more responsibility.

My job at AAIM was exciting and interesting. I ran meetings and acted as a link between a national office and branches throughout the country. It formed a solid base from which to jump—something many people in their forties strive to do.

In summing up this period of my life, I find that I learned more about survival in that period than in any other period of my life. I made two important changes in my career. It was time of great excitement for me, both on the job and at home. It was especially rewarding to be able to coordinate my personal life with my work life.

Survey Results

People in this age group are competent, can handle new jobs, and have acquired political know-how. As one of them says, "Political considerations and personal acceptability dominate your destiny as you rise in an organization or accept a new job. Most discharges at this level result from either not having enough competence or not realizing the realities of the political situation."

Two quotes illustrate the importance of goal-setting at this age:

"It is my experience that there are two things besides talent and luck that characterize success in the business community. One is a strong goal orientation that smacks of single-mindedness, and the other is having the confidence of your superior. You don't need both. The first can be sufficient if you job-hop properly. The second is a requirement for internal movement."

"There has not been too much change since I turned 40. Earlier I was more concerned with image and big money. Now I am more concerned with keeping my good reputation, providing needed quality services, and having necessary time and money to pursue my leisure pursuits."

What do people in their forties like about their current jobs?

"I have the backing of top managers. They have confidence

in my ability, I have a lot of freedom to do what I want to do, and they support my requests for new programs and projects. They are understanding and humane people."

"The diversity of responsibilities plus the opportunity to practice labor law."

"I can be of service to others. I can utilize my skills in speaking and writing. My job is results-oriented and I am a results-oriented person."

"It offers me an opportunity to apply my professional knowledge in a dynamic, open, and equitable environment."

"I like my job because it is fun! It entails the projection of new technology and invention to associated applications."

I hope that these few quotes convey the executives' enthusiasm for their jobs. They are looking for excitement and diversity; they want to run their own shows and want to provide services as well. If industry can offer all that, why not be excited about it? We spend so much time at work that it would be very grim indeed if our jobs weren't rewarding.

How would people in their forties like to see their jobs change? Their gripes include excessive travel, lack of a freewheeling atmosphere where they can carry out their ideas, lack of a supportive staff, complacent or ineffective supervisors, lack of funds for projects, and, most of all, lack of recognition. They resent it when people higher in management take the credit for their ideas. Others object to crisis management and to not having enough hours in the day to get their jobs done well.

A comment from one of the survey participants reflects the real need for recognition: "Clients tend to be unappreciative because they think money is appreciation enough." That comment, which comes from an eminently successful entrepreneur, voices a very common concern. No matter how successful one is, there is still the desire for recognition beyond money. I found this wish either explicitly stated or implied in so many of the respondents' answers. It seems that soul-searching about the job is strongest in this age group. Is the money that so many of them have acquired enough? It doesn't seem to be.

Hazards and Risks.   What are the hazards and pitfalls of getting and keeping a management position? This group's responses to that question do not differ much from the responses of other age groups, but they are verbalized more explicitly here. Managing home and the job seems to be one of the chief concerns especially for women. They find it difficult to give full attention to work commitments when a child is sick. Today, parents must cope with drug problems and other issues of a fast-moving youth culture, and they sometimes devote more worry to the family than to the job. Firms are sympathetic—up to a point. Missing an important management meeting for personal, family-related reasons doesn't set too well with management. Deciding who comes first, the family or the job, is just one of the hazards of this age group.

Another frustration lies in not being able to get to the chief executive officer or whoever makes top management decisions. In some companies, you can't make decisions on your own, but you can't reach the decision-making executive. People in this age bracket have many responsibilities and yet many of them lack the necessary clout to get into the front office unless there is an emergency. However, there is always a favored executive who gets in to see the boss without waiting. Company politics is a dangerous game—but I have yet to find a company where it isn't played.

Being in the wrong spot at the wrong time is also hazardous. If management development is a high-priority item, the labor relations superstar should move elsewhere. Political compatibility and timing are of the utmost importance. At this age, people do not fail because of incompetence, but because of timing and politics.

Mergers, acquisitions, and personnel changes can create perilous situations for executives in their forties. Their jobs are the plums coveted by ambitious young workers on their way up. If a new manager takes over, he often insists on moving in his own team, not because his people know more, but because he has worked with them successfully elsewhere.

Concern about the bottom line haunts every business. What's left after all expenses are paid? Unlike the production area's contribution, management's contribution is often hard to measure. If people aren't conscious of the bottom line, then in the long run the company will fail. People in their forties are usually anxious to assume financial responsibility for their activities. One respondent complains that he was not able to acquire such responsibilities quickly enough, and now age was catching up with him. Such concerns are motivated by the belief that if you can show that you are making money directly for the firm, your job is not often in jeopardy.

In short, the major hazards run the gamut from too little to too much trust in others, from taking too many risks to not risking enough, from blaming others to assuming full responsibility. It is not easy to pinpoint the hazards in a particular position, but each and every one who answered the survey recognized that the climb up the management ladder is not an easy one. Family concerns are pressing. Playing politics can't be avoided. Keeping abreast of new information is a formidable task. If you are lucky enough to be in your vigorous instead of your beaten forties, you can handle all these potential pitfalls. If events at one job are impossible to live with, you still have time to move—and many people do in their forties.

Work Records. Let's look at the work records of the people in their forties. Upward movement is a distinguishing feature of this age group. Over half of the respondents had three to four jobs before becoming a vice-president or a director of production. Others stayed with one firm and were promoted from one job to a higher one. Those who move to different firms hear of better opportunitites through search firms, a unique phenomenom of our age, or through friends in the industry or other personal contacts.

One person, who runs an outstanding labor relations firm, spent one semester working as an English teacher before becoming a union organizer for the International Brotherhood of Electrical Workers. In his next job, he switched sides from union to management and became an employee of a management labor relations consulting firm. I know several executives who made the same transition. Interestingly, I have never seen someone move from the management side to the union.

The president reports that he left teaching to work for the union as a lark, but that his change to management consulting had more serious motivations. He wanted to learn more about the field, and was becoming dissatisfied with his old job. Now he is working for himself, which has meant independence and more money. He says this when asked about the turning points in his career: "I was lucky enough to be hired by the union when they thought I had a master's in industrial relations. If they had known I was an english major—no chance! I was lucky enough to have met one of the true geniuses of labor relations early in my career. I ended out a bad marriage and have a very good one in its place; my wife has supported me every step of the way!"

Another respondent spent three years working for someone else, and then started his own actuarial consultant firm, an arrangement which he finds very satisfying.

The lack of opportunity with management in the old spot versus the increase in potential opportunities in the new job were the main reasons given for the change of jobs. Increased salary was also very important. Again, this goes along with the thesis that executives in their forties will leave a job if better opportunities with more pay are available.

Changing jobs is still a risky business, particularly if you have a high salary and lots of responsibilities. No two jobs are exactly alike and if you expect to move into a comfortable spot that will be similar to your old security blanket, you will be rudely awakened. Regardless of the enthusiasm of recruiters and top management, moving into a new position is not easy. On the whole, however, the participants in the survey are willing to take risks in order to get the freedom of action they desire.

The people surveyed found new jobs mainly through recruiters (headhunters) or personal contacts, or a combination of the two. Only one person found a job through an advertisement; one other used self-promotion letters. Most of those surveyed agree that sending resumes out "cold" is not a very productive way to find a new top-flight position. In general, when an executive (no matter how old) decides it's time to find a new job, he or she should be prepared to do a careful, exacting job of looking. Every possible resource should be used in searching for a new position. I am still appalled at the haphazard fashion that most executives apply to this task. There is no guarantee that any one method will always produce the best results. However, the systematic, thorough use of a variety of tactics will usually pay off. So, to say that sending resumes is unnecessary or that headhunters should be ignored is just not wise. I have seen executives get plum jobs through strange avenues. A casual airplane conversation can change the direction of your life. An ad in *The Wall Street Journal* may provide you with just the spot you want. A friend who respects your abilities may be the key. And if your own company knows there is no advancement for you there, it may help you find a position somewhere else—but don't count on it too much. Chances are (and the survey does bear this out) your old bosses are probably just as restless with you as you are with them.

Attitudes toward Age. People in this group have formulated opinions about different periods in their lives. The following comments indicate their attitudes and advice about youth, middle age, and retirement:

> *Youth:* "Get as much education as you can and enjoy a good social life at school."
>
> *Middle life:* "A good marriage partner with whom one can communicate is most important. I feel sorry for men who say they can't take their business problems home. They are estranged from their wives. Also, maintain good communication with your children. Finally, involve yourself in community affairs: get on the school board, hospital board, and so on. Try to pay society back for what it has done for you."
>
> "I have always had a difficult time dealing with the question of age. I like to quote Satchel Paige (the seemingly ageless minor league baseball player) who said,

'You are as old as you think you would be if you didn't know how old you were.' "

"Youth should be a time to try many things without worrying about security; a time to find your niche. Middle years should be the time to build your career and become proficient at what you do. Old age should be the time to enjoy what you've worked for—to work or loaf or do whatever your heart desires."

"*Always* strive for the freedom to explore the unknown—no age limit."

The observations and advice given above range from the ever-young approach to age to the more traditional view of old age as a time to relax. Interestingly, those in the survey who are over 60 are more inclined to want to "die in the harness." Those now in their forties believe they will be relieved to leave the work world behind them.

In a somewhat related question, Table 3 shows how

Table 3. Importance of selected factors on success of people in their forties.

	Very Important	Important	Unimportant
Education	50%	40%	10%
Upbringing and Friends	20%	30%	50%
Marriage and Family		50%	50%
Mentors or Role Models	20%	50%	30%
Supervisors or Superiors	40%	50%	10%
Personal Interests	50%	20%	30%
Mergers and Acquisitions	40%	10%	40%

they assess the importance of certain factors in their success. (Numbers indicate the percent of respondents who checked the answer.)

Note that education was very important for this group. Marriage and family, while important, do not overshadow other factors. People in this group assign greater importance to mentors and supervisors than people in older groups do. For all age groups, personal interests played an important role. Additional factors mentioned by respondents include personal ambitions, aggressiveness in pursuing career goals, developing management skills, and establishing a track record.

Do's and Don'ts.   What advice do people in their forties have for us? They emphasize the importance of learning and improving communication skills: writing, speaking, and listening. They encourage you to choose employers carefully and thoroughly and to look over the field before changing jobs. Staying in good physical shape is advocated (in fact, there are a number of joggers in this group). They acknowledge the importance of having a competent staff, and of passing along recognition to deserving subordinates. This group feels that real strength comes from teamwork, and managers are encouraged to delegate properly. They urge others to be budget conscious and to respect the importance of the bottom line.

They urge others not to lie, stagnate, or double-deal. Don't be self-centered or opinionated, and don't expect instant rewards. Finally, they warn people not to become part of gossip and rumor grapevines.

A list of don'ts that is a little salty bears reprinting. It includes:

1. Don't kiss the boss's ass.
2. Don't worry about being fired.

3. Don't be ruled by money.
4. Don't drink too much.
5. Don't do things just because others are doing them.
6. Don't ignore your gut feelings.
7. Don't spend all your time in meetings.
8. Don't put the corporation ahead of the family.
9. Don't get caught.

Remember, these respondents are executives who have strived for success. But they have maintained what seems to me to be a fairly decent set of ethics. The "don't get caught" comment, although probably made facetiously, has more truth to it than most of us like to admit. Almost every executive I know has made plenty of mistakes. Sometimes it is better to report an error, but sometimes it's better to remedy the situation yourself. That is, of course, if it is not so major that the business will fall apart because of it. The boss probably doesn't want to be bothered with your minor mistakes; he or she expects you to correct them. Don't embarrass the brass by being caught looking foolish or, worse yet, by making the boss look incompetent. This advice is only for the competent executive who understands what I am talking about. This doesn't apply to being caught with your hand in the till or to making major mistake after major mistake. I do mean that you should use your head about both your own and your subordinate's frailties.

Conclusion. I found this particular age group especially lively. Their comments and their outlook reflect the enthusiasm of their age. Competent, ambitious, looking for the right spot, the respondents to the questionnaire are, I believe, a fair representation of executives in their forties.

Case Study: Mary Sutter, Vice-President of a Major Bank

Mary Sutter is one of the most interesting people I have encountered. She is in her early forties and holds a top management job. She maintains a fine relationship with her family, partly as a result of her husband, who is very supportive. Like many women in important jobs, she took a very short maternity leave. In fact, Mary dealt with some very ticklish company matters a few days after the birth of her son.

She learned the "virtues" of hard work early in life. She pays warm tribute to her parents, who saw to it that she received a fine education. (Much of her education was gained through scholarships and by attending night school.) She is typical of nearly everyone interviewed in recognizing the importance of education and doing something about attaining it. Mary had to work hard to obtain the education she needed for the job she now holds. Today, younger women in their twenties and thirties take it for granted that they can be as well educated as men. But it has not always been so easy. Just ask Mary or me.

Her parents were a real help to her through their support of her career aims. Many current books emphasize that the early childhood role for girls lays much of the groundwork for their future careers. My friend had the best of both worlds. She learned to cook and sew, but was also taught early to think, analyze, and make decisions.

Like many other executives in their forties, she knows the importance of cultivating a wide range of interests. She enjoys both music and interior decorating. In addition, both she and her husband sing professionally. She is an avid tennis player and likes skiing and other sports.

Her career path indicates both stamina and a willingness to take risks. She started work as a stenographer and moved up through the secretarial ranks while going to school at night. Because of her understanding of people and her managerial ability, she was soon training other secretaries. Eventually, she moved on to personnel and equal employment opportunity (EEO) work.

Her stories about the way she was interviewed for jobs would make an enlightened executive shudder. Like many other women, she ran into the old saw about the feasibility of traveling. What would her husband's reaction be? Could she handle driving at night? She received smaller raises than men in similar spots, because the men were "heads of families."

She has learned the lessons of management well. She recognizes the importance of developing subordinates, of giving credit where credit is due, and of not passing the buck. Like many other executives, she grows impatient with the extensive paperwork attached to management positions and finds it hard to tolerate incompetent or sloppy work.

She wonders where her path will lead. She believes that women are more insecure than men, that we are not so sure of our capabilities. And yet, we want to make the most of our many talents. She is a capable, ambitious, and sensitive woman who knows her field. She's a good supervisor who also relates well to top management. She typifies, as so many in the survey do, the drive and concern of people in their forties.

5

The Fifties—

Years of Panic, Distress,

and Survival

Overview

If you can survive the critical years of the fifties, then you can probably carry on until retirement. This is the time when all your mistakes catch up with you. If you haven't made the proper management decisions by age 50, the roof comes falling in. In addition, the grim statistics of the obituary page show the heart victims, the ulcer victims, and the all-too-sudden deaths in this age group. "He was too young to die," is the sad comment of executive peers. "He worked too hard. It finally caught up with him," is another comment heard too often.

If you can hang on until 60, it seems that the company is willing to tolerate you until retirement. "We can't get rid of old Joe. He only has a few more years until he retires. He's a long-service employee, and how would it look if we kicked him out now?" No such benevolence for the executive in his or her fifties. If departments are falling down in production, if deadlines for reports aren't met, or if there is a general shake-up, the company will have no compunction about kicking out a 50-year-old.

What else does the person of 50 have to worry about in corporate structure other than sudden death and lagging work records? Mergers and acquisitions—the bugaboo of the aging executive. Before and immediately after a merger, management shrilly contends that no one will be lost in the shuffle. It's not too long, however, before you hear terms like *attrition* and *overstaffing*. That's the crisis situation that makes the executive of 50 sweat until he or she finds out whether or not the ax is going to fall this time.

Sometimes the company will help a displaced executive find another job. Management may furnish an office with secretarial and phone service for a few months, or even pay for outplacement. The new outplacement firms are a sign of the times. Twenty years ago they were unheard of; today, they are often swamped with 50-year-old executives who have been "let go." Unemployment hits these people especially hard. They are used to working regularly and living well, and they have families to support. Often, the sacked employee just can't admit to himself or herself, let alone to the family, that the job isn't there any more. More than one ex-employee doesn't tell the family until absolutely necessary. In some sad cases, people will take the same train each day and come home at the regular time, pretending that they're still employed. When the ax falls, almost all are poorly informed about how to pick up the pieces and look for another job. Once they have found another job, it is difficult to make the adjustment and to start over.

There are exceptions to this unhappy group. Many competent executives who have been forced out of their jobs by circumstances have called on their courage and good common sense to help find positions equal to or better than the ones they left.

Two cases studies, one illustrating courage and one foresight, may help to show that successful changes can be made—in spite of age and rough times.

Jane Brown was the vice-president of personnel of a prestigious firm that employed approximately 300 people. She had been with the firm for over 12 years, starting out as personnel director and moving up to vice-president, a position she had held for five years. She encountered stiff competition in decision making—a new president tried to second-guess Jane on all personnel problems and plans. Then, the president used signs of an economic downturn as an excuse to abolish the personnel department. Of course, Jane's fate was the same as her department's. This situation developed over a period of time, but there was absolutely no warning to individuals who were sacked. Most had built reputations that were above reproach. The firings were sudden and swift, which added to the brutality of the situation.

My friend, who was told about being caught in the cut of employees on her way home from a company executive dance, brought herself up short from her first devastating week of self-pity. She focused her brilliant executive abilities on the task of marketing herself to potential employers. A self-analysis of skills and a review of accomplishments (and of a few weaknesses) convinced her that she could get a job. She was lucky to have the support of family and friends throughout this difficult time. Her indomitable will triumphed, and she has found a new executive home and is now extremely pleased.

Jack Johnson made a voluntary move. He looked at his job and found he was bored to death. He was tired of working in a small town for a fairly small firm, and saw only limited promotion opportunities ahead. He wanted to work in executive hiring and placement in a bigger firm, where he could not only study the in-house promotables but also handle college recruiting. It's not easy to sell yourself when you are over 50, and Jack's job was even harder—he wanted to become a college recruiter! However, he put together an effective "sales" package of himself, which included a resume and demonstrations of his past accomplishments. He was choosy, and it took him about seven months to find what he was looking for. But once he found the right job, he stayed there until he retired at age 65. He was proud of the fact that his college recruitment record was better than those of younger recruiters.

Too often, however, executives give up too soon. When someone asks, "Whatever happened to Joe?" the answer is, "I saw him around for a while, but he just seems to have evaporated into thin air." Sometimes long afterward you'll hear he is making jewelry in Florida and his wife is working. The world doesn't have to fall apart for you in your fifties, but be aware that this is a time of dirty tricks in the corporate jungle. People do survive and prosper, as both my own experiences and those of the 22 survey participants in this group attest, but it takes alertness, perseverence, and dedication.

My Fifties

Unlike some of the people in the survey, I was secure during my fifties. Because of my past successes, I was able to pick and choose where I wanted to be. At 49, I became vice-president of the National Metal Trades Association, which had specialized in job evaluation for many years. My job entailed planning and running meetings, which I had done at American Management Associations. I had been sought for the job, which made moving there easier. I had an excellent, innovative boss, whom I had worked for at AMA and who knew both my strengths and my weaknesses. My assistant from AMA moved with me, which gave me the kind of support I needed. In addition, the job built on my strengths, namely, disseminating information and running top-flight meetings. My ability to find talented people who were willing to share their information with NMTA members was probably my greatest contribution.

The Association grew and attracted members from banks, chemical concerns, insurance companies, and glass companies. Because of this, the name of the organization was changed to the American Association of Industrial Management.

Just as in many other work situations, AAIM began to make changes. Changes can be good, but they can also alter job responsibilities. Such changes can play havoc with one's well-laid plans. If you are to survive you must stay flexible, but if the situation keeps getting worse and you cannot control it, then it's time to start looking, no matter what age you are.

What had been a safe haven became so unstable that I felt it best to look elsewhere. The following sequence of events led me to leave the AAIM when I was 57. The Association made a costly investment in buildings for headquarters, there was lack of cooperation among branches, I was absent from headquarters, and, finally, my boss left AAIM for a job in academia.

Fortunately or unfortunately, work situations are often extremely fluid. I have always felt that certain people are essential to hold an organization together. Some people can be replaced, but work relationships are like a jigsaw puzzle: take one piece away and it's awfully hard to find another piece that will fit in its place. The circumstances described above, especially the departure of my boss, created hazards that I was forced to deal with.

I began to look for another spot, and I discovered some very interesting opportunities. I found that reevaluating my career in my late fifties was not a hopeless task. In fact, I was able to choose from several fine opportunities, and finally decided to accept a job as vice-president of personnel of the National Retail Merchants Association.

The pluses were that the salary was the best offer, a special retirement plan was set up for me, association work had been my forte for a long time, my experience in personnel work was long and varied, and my assistant made the move with me. However, there were hazards: I really knew little about the intricacies of retailing. I replaced a gentleman who had run the personnel division for 40 years. When replacing a competent person, everyone expects you to do things the way George did them. Any new methods must be explained and must prove successful.

Fortunately, NRMA was a fine place to work. The cooperation of store executives, NRMA peers, and top management was outstanding. While I worked there, NRMA underwent a management shuffle, but both my assistant and I survived—possibly because we had the job well in hand and did not become involved in political fighting. Also, we were not quite at the top, which can often be a more hazardous place when major changes are made.

Needless to say, the first days were hectic, and from the beginning until the time I left, the job never stopped being hectic. With over 55,000 stores around the world, I was the "maven" in personnel. Because the job was interesting and exciting, I found that I was not restless. I began to think that perhaps I was getting old enough to stay with one job (a feeling I shared with other people in their late fifties). In fact, I remained at NRMA until retirement—a record for me: 9½ years on one job.

How do I compare with the respondents to the survey, who are now in that magic transition period of their lives?

Survey Results

All but four of the respondents have at least one college degree; five have MBAs. If executives now in their twenties were to be surveyed when they become 50, we would probably find that all of them have college degrees and several have doctorates.

Most of those surveyed are married, and many report that they have children in college. They're looking forward to the time when this heavy financial burden will be lifted. Then, they say, they might be able to "live their own lives." Outside financial pressures keep more than a few people, especially those in their fifties, glued to one spot.

Among those surveyed in this age group are several vice-presidents, three senior vice-presidents, two presidents, a factory superintendent, consultants, trade association executives, and a few personnel directors. Almost all have had four or five jobs before their current ones. Five have risen steadily up the management ladder in one firm; the other 17 have changed firms. One woman stayed home until her children were grown and then went back to work, and one man now combines a clergyman's role with that of consultant.

Some people mention that if they had their lives to live over again they would try to get better acquainted with their firms earlier, and, especially, they would try to get more education. One person wishes he had studied law. The increasing government regulations and the legal implications of many management situations have made such knowledge almost a prerequisite for some management jobs.

Career Goals. How have their attitudes toward their careers differed at different times in their lives? Most of them realized the importance of really doing a good job early in their careers in order to form a basis for their future successes. Not many took time "finding themselves," as we sometimes find younger people doing now. In order to further their careers, most were willing to move less frequently in their fifties than they did in their earlier years. As one respondent put it, "In my early thirties, career was more important than family or stability. In my early forties, family and stability, particularly in terms of my children's education, became more important than changing jobs to advance career. Now I want to stay put." The clergyman, who had once been a business executive, puts it this way, "My concepts have not changed appreciably now that I am in my fifties, except that my subsequent studies and ordination as a clergyman have probably provided me with more internal stability and competence to cope with reverses while maintaining an optimistic outlook."

Changing Jobs: Pros and Cons. Why did the respondents change jobs? What were the enticements? Here are a few of the answers.

Lack of opportunity in a job drove more than one person to seek employment elsewhere. The green grass on the other side of the fence offers additional responsibility and increased freedom of action. Often added to that is the opportunity for more managerial activity rather than supervisory functions. High on everyone's list, including my own, is the opportunity to make more money. A phenomenon of the current executive scene is that a firm will neglect the genius on its own staff, paying just the going salary, but will hire someone from the outside (who may or may not be better) at a much higher salary. However, one respondent says that after you make $50,000 or more, money isn't such a lure. The job itself, according to him, then takes on more importance.

What mistakes have people made in their job changes? Some say none. Career planning at an early age seems to have been rare, but there are a few respondents who say they are exactly where they planned to be. One person says that he knows there are increased opportunities in New York, but that his wife refuses to move there. (We hear from young people these days about how important climate and location are; my friend's wife seems to have been ahead of her time.) A vice-president of a bank in a cold northern city says he'd like a similar position where it is warmer. In this respect, people in their fifties are not much different from younger people who place emphasis on where they are going to live and the lifestyle they want. However, executives in their fifties probably have more money to indulge a preference than young people do. People who are just starting out must sometimes make personal concessions to obtain a high-paying, interesting job.

There seems to be a corporate trend toward moving from the heart of big cities to rural or suburban areas. One person examines the effect of such moves on executives: "When the scene shifts from large cities to small towns, the interoffice and executive-suite climate changes radically, as do social and civic interrelationships with superiors, peers, and subordinates. It is one thing to work with other people for eight or more hours a day and see them only at work. It is quite another thing to be involved with the same people socially, politically, and even residentially 24 hours a day, 365 days a year." This is particularly true when one's management stature in the company imposes civic responsibilities. For example, it's not uncommon to find the personnel director appointed chairman of the town finance committee; the research director, chairman of the board of education; the chief engineer, chairman of public works. And the wives of executives often become chairperson of the PTA, chairwoman of the hospital auxiliary, and so on.

Do they have regrets about the professional moves they have made? A few do. One questions the long-term wisdom of leaving a company to accept a substantially better offer. "Had I stayed, I feel my long-range advancement would probably have been significantly greater. Upon reflection, subsequent mistakes probably stemmed from the same cause—precipitous decisions and actions."

It is interesting that no one places the blame of his or her mistakes on the shoulders of any other person. Some blame circumstances such as mergers or new, unappreciative management, but no one specifically blames a terrible ogre of a boss. As I mentioned in Chapter 4, I moved once because I thought my boss was incompetent. I found I couldn't work for anyone who I thought made all the wrong decisions both for himself, for the company, and, especially, for me. Maybe I am not as nice as the respondents to the questionnaire, but I am sure that the character of one's boss has more to do with management changes than many people are willing to admit.

What prevents people in their fifties from changing jobs? Even though most respondents said that workers over 55 do not pay more attention to retirement than they do to the jobs, they do admit that age plays a significant role in their reluctance to change jobs. Mental outlook can become a real hazard as far as worker advancement or change are concerned. Personal lifestyle is often important, too. Home situations and spouses' careers also figure in the decision of whether or not to change jobs.

Over half of those surveyed look forward to keeping their current positions until retirement. Perhaps this attitude will change in the future, if 70 becomes the more common retirement age.

Concerns. There was one woman included in this age group of the survey. She learned the hard way that women still have a battle to fight in gaining recognition in upper-management ranks. Today, younger women have a head start up the ladder, and probably won't be as frustrated when they are 50. We hope that unfounded sex-related prejudices will have disappeared by then.

When it comes to changing jobs, a high salary requirement can deter a company from hiring an older executive. The company assumes that if it forces an applicant to take a lower paying and often less challenging job, he or she will be dissatisfied. (And that's probably the case.) Others are worried about keeping up with rapid changes in today's world. For example, what they learn about computers is outdated within a very short time. They are reluctant to take time off from their jobs to become updated. On the other hand, young people are more apt to go back to school or take special classes in order to keep up.

Domestic problems are another concern of people in

this group. More breakups occur in long-term marriages at this period, often because the executive's wife has become disillusioned with her role. Perhaps younger women, who plan to have careers as well as marriages, will manage each phase of their lives more carefully than their mothers, who limited their roles to the traditional ones of wife and mother.

Several respondents recognized that they had grown rigid in their opinions—a trait not reserved to people in their fifties, but more prevalent among older executives.

Finally, some reported that they had received much responsibility, possibly because of their increasing gray hairs, but had received neither corresponding pay nor authority.

We asked how important certain factors had been in the careers of people in this group. Table 4 shows a breakdown of their responses.

Table 4. Importance of selected factors on success of people in their fifties.

	Very Important	Important	Unimportant
Education	40%	50%	10%
Upbringing and Friends	25%	25%	50%
Marriage and Family	20%	50%	30%
Mentors or Role Models	50%	10%	40%
Supervisors or Superiors	45%	45%	10%
Personal Interests	50%	30%	20%
Mergers and Acquisitions	10%	40%	50%

Note the heavy emphasis on education. The respondents who indicated that this factor was unimportant made it in the business world without college degrees. However, they are making sure that their children receive as fine an education as possible. The respondents feel that marriage and family play an important role. Personal interests rank very high among the listed factors. This is of special interest because it indicates a trend toward integration of work and personal life. Note, too, that most give credit to their mentors and supervisors. Several respondents suggested additional factors, such as extra hard work, professional association, and plain blind luck (both good and bad).

Advice. Here is this group's advice to others about getting and keeping a management job:

1. Get a broad-based education.
2. Avoid occupational over-specialization (such as cost accountant or time-study engineer)
3. Learn all possible areas of the operation.
4. Continue your education, either formally or by personal research, reading, or studies.
5. Objectively evaluate the political climate of your company.
6. Accept criticism and make constructive changes.
7. Adapt to changing conditions.
8. Keep abreast of advancements in your own occupational field.
9. Cultivate supportive social contacts.
10. Establish and maintain a personal code of ethical behavior.
11. Don't become known for thinking up ways of dissipating the company's resources.

12. Don't have an excuse for everything and blame others regularly.
13. Don't take all the credit—after all, you don't deserve it.
14. Don't surround yourself with lovely people who aren't bright.

A comment worth noting from a senior vice-president: "I have seen a distinct trend toward government intervention in the employee–employer relationship, which has created a situation in which the employer has no choices." Many executives in their fifties are concerned about government intervention. As one man expressed it: "The young executive never questions a government form. It is an expected procedure so they fill out anything the government asks for. I get very upset and think most of the stuff is none of their business and fill out only what is absolutely mandatory—and I gripe about that, too. It is a different world and it discourages me."

Conclusion. People in this group are proud of their records, but somewhat fearful of the times and unforeseen circumstances. They know that they may have a rough time finding a demand for their skills elsewhere, unless they are recruited to new jobs by outside sources and leave their old jobs voluntarily. That doesn't mean, however, that these people will not change jobs. If the incentive exists, they have no reluctance to try something new. When asked whether they had failed on any jobs they undertook, the answer was a unanimous "No." They believe that since they haven't failed in the past, they won't do so in the future.

The fifties are treacherous in the management world, but with care the traps can be avoided and careers can be fulfilled. I see little evidence of the Peter Principle among the respondents. As one respondent expressed it, "In my fifties I feel the confidence gained from my experience." Two examples of successful career people now in their fifties help illustrate the trends observed in this chapter. Both case studies are typical of the points we have discussed above about this particular age group.

Case Study: James Miller,
President of His Own Search Firm
Connie Miller,
Executive Vice-President and Treasurer

An interesting joint interview with Connie (in her forties) and James (in his early fifties) revealed some new concepts and supported the views of other survey participants. James is president and Connie is executive vice-president and treasurer of a successful executive search firm.

Both James and Connie had a varied work experience and changed jobs several times before launching their own firm three years ago. Connie says she thinks she was born working. While she was in high school, she worked as a dime-store clerk and managed the books for a dancing school. After graduating from Dickinson College in Pennsylvania she went to California, where she worked in both personnel and public relations for a company. Her next job was in the personnel department of an educational organization, where she spent several years. She then moved to a manufacturing company, where she broadened her personnel experience to include labor relations. When her particular group dissolved, she became involved in compensation and evaluation. Rather than move with the company when it relocated its headquarters, she left to work with an association in New York. Shortly afterward there was a management shake-up, and she remained on that job for only six months. She then went into executive search work, which she has been successful at and which she enjoys very much.

Her husband, James, also made several career changes before he established their firm. In his first job, he worked as a delivery man for his family's business. His performance there was uneven and he left under tumultuous circumstances. (He inadvertently backed a laundry truck into the president's Cadillac and wrecked another parked car.) As he put it, "I quit before I got fired."

He received his B.A. and M.A. from Penn State and then joined the Air Force where he became a flyer and also worked as a personnel officer at Randolph Field. After leaving the Air Force, he became personnel director of a manufacturing firm, and then moved to another company to become industrial relations director. He worked for the two companies for a total of 13 years. When the second company was sold, he left to become personnel director for a larger firm in New York City, which gave him international as well as national experience in personnel. He refused a promotion which would have meant moving to Paris, and left that company to work for another. There he broadened his experience to include labor relations in a unionized firm. Just as his wife had, he left the firm rather than move outside of New York when the headquarters were moved to an out-of-the-way town.

He then became a partner in a search firm, where he remained until the founding of his own firm with Connie three years ago. Together, they have found a very special niche in the management world.

The experience of these two individuals illustrates the

flexibility required to reach desired management goals. They moved from firm to firm in order to move upward—one of the types of career paths discussed in this book. Other people move up the ladder in one or perhaps two firms. There is no one road to the top. Success requires professional ability and a willingness to change and to learn. Both James and Connie consider these characteristics to be important not only to them, but also to the executives they interview and help place.

What do they and the many executives they have helped place consider to be important factors in getting and keeping a management job? At the top of everyone's list is the chance to take on new challenges and be involved in a continuous learning experience. Executives want smooth working relations, and will leave a job if a new leader doesn't speak their language or does not have the team spirit they are used to.

6

The Sixties—

Time of Adjustment

Overview

The working world of the sixties is a time of contrasting views. Just as there are myths about other special groups of workers, such as women or ethnic minorities, there are many myths about older workers. Among the myths are:

Old workers are slow and can't meet production standards.

Old workers can't meet the physical demands of the job.

Old workers can't be depended on—they're absent from work too often.

Old workers are not adaptable—they won't accept change.

Hiring old workers increases pension and insurance costs.

Numerous studies have proved that there is no significant drop in productivity with increasing age and that less than 1 percent of today's jobs require great strength or heavy lifting. In fact, labor-saving machinery makes it possible for older workers to handle most jobs without difficulty. Although workers over 60 may be subject to health problems, many take better care of themselves than most young people do. As a group, older workers have an excellent record. Studies also show that people in their sixties are flexible in accepting changes in their occupations and earnings. Adaptability does depend on the individual: many young people are set in their ways, and many older employees adjust to change readily. Higher costs in retirement and other benefit plans are more than offset by the low turnover rate among older workers and by the high quality of their work.

There is little correlation between a manager's age and corporate performance. Individual performance, not age, should be the basis for moving people out. Many people have remained active and effective throughout their later years. For example, George Meany didn't retire until he was 86; he was in his prime when he was in his sixties.

Nevertheless, some younger workers resent the individual who remains on the job after age 60, as indicated by the following remarks.

"My boss was a military leader and as such he cannot escape his background. He just won't accept new ideas or reforms easily."

(There are many semiretired or retired military officers who are in upper management today. I would hesitate to say that the above boss is typical.)

"I can't be promoted because there are too many senior people ahead of me. Many are over 60 and it looks as though they will stay where they are until they are 70 because of the new law. If that's the case, I'll have to move where the lines are unplugged. I can't wait five or ten more years."

How does this attitude differ from the way we viewed old people when I was young? That was a long time ago. At that time, life expectancy was shorter, grandmothers and grandfathers were part of the family household, women remained at home, and people who worked past the age of 60 were usually professionals such as doctors, ministers, or professors. We were very respectful of old people; however, we weren't in direct competition with them for jobs. I know that my working friends who are over 60 feel that they are as good as or better than the people who are waiting around for their jobs.

Nevertheless, younger, aggressive employees do feel their progress is blocked by an older person's retention of a key spot. A poll of graduate students at the universities where I have been teaching during the past 20 years indicates that the primary concern of a majority of students is that there is no spot to move upward to as long as the "old man" or "old woman" keeps working.

How do older people feel about this?

"There are always people on the ladder below you who are pushing upward and it should not be surprising you'd be asked to make way for younger talent. That is what happened to me, and it wasn't a happy moment. It brought on a consciousness of my age and disability."

This is one person's version of what happened to him as he approached his sixtieth birthday. Is everyone affected? Is work really so different after you have reached this "advanced" age? It all depends. As one of my friends put it: "When you are 60 you have accumulated a lot of knowledge and are still healthy enough to enjoy life." I'd be inclined to agree.

My Sixties

For me, the time between 60 and 65 was basically a happy and prosperous time. My vice-presidency at NRMA brought with it several of the hazards discussed above, but it was a productive, successful period of my work career. It was a happy and fairly prosperous time. I saw no diminution of duties or respect and, even with no great increase in earnings, it was a very satisfactory period.

For me, the sixtieth birthday did indeed come as a shock. I was very busy with my job and outside interests and commitments. I suddenly realized that people thought I was an old-timer. Society has decided that 60-year-olds are entering the "Golden Age." Then I realized how lucky I was to still have a demanding job, a supportive family, and fine friends both in and out of the industrial world.

There are certain times when people take stock, and age 60 is one of those times. I found myself reassessing my career and my goals. I had changed jobs at 57 and was still finding the world challenging, but should I again start keeping my ears open for new challenges, should I consider switching jobs? At age 57 I had suddenly realized that I had no pension plan and, even with a fair amount of savings, I would be facing a bleak old age. I remedied that by taking a job with a company that provided excellent retirement and pension benefits. I decided I would really try to stay content in that job until I retired—and retirement seemed, at that time, to be in the distant future. Incidentally, between age 60 and my retirement at age 65, I was tempted by two good job offers, both of which I turned down. Was the decision to stay the right one? Who knows?

What are the advantages of working after 60? You'll probably be considered an "authority" in your field. If you have done an excellent job until then, you have little danger of anyone really catching up to you in knowledge, not only of the work itself, but of the vagaries of the people with whom you work.

The pressures are there, however, and you must work to maintain your position on the mountaintop. If you stay alert, keep current, play your politics right, stay healthy, work like a trooper, and don't ask for favors because you are old, there is no reason why you should fear the young pusher or, sometimes, the old peer who is ready to grab some of your turf. If you have the misfortune of ill health, and too often ailments occur between ages 60 and 70, then you must of necessity make concessions and plan less or no work. Some of the saddest cases we know are people who were forced to leave work because of illness. Some of the lucky ones recovered and were welcomed back, but never to the same place of power. Others, however, were forced to drop out of the race for good, occasionally at management's demand.

I was healthy in my sixties and could maintain the same vigorous schedule I had regularly pursued: working, teaching, writing, and keeping house. It is important that you keep your schedule, even if you do have a few more aches and pains than you had before.

After you are 60, it becomes harder to watch management disasters occur. You'll often be forced to go along with a management decision which you know has no chance of working. It's hard not to say "I told you so" when the inevitable happens.

During my last year of work before retirement I began to grow more nostalgic about work. I became more aware of its importance to me and of the fact that it was bound to end. Fortunately, I had decided long before that I didn't want to stop working and made specific plans for the future. This is much easier to do while you're still working than after you leave, when facilities and people are not so readily available. It's a change that you can foresee and can do something about.

Because management assumes you won't be around much longer, you are left out of far-reaching plans for the future. You find that peers or even subordinates are called in for the planning you used to be consulted about. Sure it hurts, but you may as well be realistic about life, particularly at your age. Chances are that the changes won't really affect you, so perhaps it's just as well you aren't involved.

In addition, management often has the temerity to assume that over-60 employees are "safe," that they are too worried about their pensions to leave. As a result, salary increases that would ordinarily be awarded to younger workers are grudgingly (and slowly) given to older workers. Has it happened to you? You know you really should get as much as or more than the younger person who will probably replace you. Unfortunately, however, employees are not always paid what they deserve.

I am told that every firm has a certain number of has-beens—people who once were great managers but now are buried in unimportant jobs. Management doesn't have the heart to make arrangements for the departure of old Joe or Martha before their official retirement date. Every working person I know who's over 60 says, "Preserve me from such a fate—it's worse than death."

However, losing a job after age 60, for whatever reason, is traumatic. When management goes on the kick of hiring a new team, which most often means a young team, the older people who lose their jobs often find it hard to get organized and begin the process of getting a new one. There is nothing worse than feeling like a discarded piece of management trash.

To survive in the management race until you are past 60 is a feat to be proud of. You can, as I have, look back at your near-misses and at your successes. Changing jobs, working with hard-to-work-with people, and completing projects on time takes a lot of stamina. It means taking care of yourself, eating and drinking less (even on business excursions), and keeping alert all the time. Don't stop just because either you or someone else thinks you are getting old.

Survey Results

There are 20 people in this age group of the survey. Only one is a woman. She is senior vice-president of personnel in a retail store. But if you conducted a similar survey 20 years from now, you'd probably find many more women among the respondents. Two people left manufacturing to become college professors, one is a plant manager in heavy industry, two are in the insurance business, one is a farmer, one works for the government, and the rest are scattered among other industries, from banking to chemicals. Six founded their own businesses when they were in their late fifties or early sixties. Most of those surveyed seem happy and busy. The majority of respondents want to keep working after retirement. One says, "I don't believe in mandatory retirement at any age, so I plan to continue what I'm doing." Another plans to "stay in harness and expand by incorporating with others." A few say they would like to phase work out and go a little slower, making some concessions to age.

Only one person says that he plans to "go fishin'." For this particular gentleman, life has been good on the job, but he is looking forward to a new and different life when he retires. He has enjoyed a successful career. Although he might have wished to become a president rather than a vice-president, he says he is "satisfied with [his] present feeling of accomplishment and contribution." He feels that he might have gone further, but had to consider his own personality and character—he is honest and outspoken. He has no regrets, for without these characteristics he wouldn't have been able to sleep easy. Like so many other people, he is appalled when there is poor selection of officers or other management personnel. Too often, the knowledgable incumbent who is over 60 is not considered for high-level jobs. A poor selection leads only to costly turnover.

Most of the respondents are extremely interested in their current jobs, saying that they offer diversity, challenges, and the opportunity to be innovative and to influence corporate policy. One person believes that her job is really worthwhile; she receives the greatest satisfaction from improving the morale of the people who work for her and likes to see them move ahead. Many people in their sixties do not have the strong driving ambition to keep moving up the management ladder. They focus that energy on training younger workers and on helping them move ahead.

One respondent admits that he made a mistake, and still suffers from a hasty decision to take a new job a year ago. Unfortunately, the new company is, in his words, a "shyster outfit." It's harder to leave a job at age 63 than it is at age 20, 30, 40, or even 50, so he stays.

Concerns. What are people in this group concerned about? Time management, obsolescence, ignorance on the part of ownership, and fatigue. They are also worried about having to make decisions in areas that they really aren't knowledgable about. In addition, they feel there is not enough time to keep up with the myriad of new inventions. For example, most of them are bewildered by the computer. They wonder if it is as accurate as their old methods. Why are the computers bought last year already obsolete? The world of computers seems to move too fast for them. Many of them betray a trace of envy when they concede that, "Young people grew up with the computer." (They are still distressed, however, by young workers' lack of knowledge about basic math, and claim they can spot errors faster than some people who take computer printouts as gospel.)

Six people in this group successfully founded their own businesses, and they all regret, as one said, that they "didn't do it a dozen years earlier."

Would most of those who answered the questionnaire change jobs? "Yes, but it would take a much higher salary and I still would want a challenging spot."

Turning Points. What were the factors that made them leave one spot and go to another? Remember, people in this group were coming of age during World War II and many were shaken from the ordinary way of life by a stint in the Army, Navy, or Air Force. The G.I. bill, which allowed people to continue their education after the service, was a real asset to many. Increased opportunity, higher salaries and better benefits in new jobs, increased funds, and greater personal satisfaction were the carrots that lured these people, as well as others in the survey, off to new jobs.

What were the other major factors affecting these people in their early jobs? Working for a boss interested in not only his own career but also the careers of subordinates, changing from local to national exposure, marrying a supportive mate, becoming specialized in one area rather than generalizing in the field were all mentioned. One reported being fired from a job for which he really was unsuited. After dusting himself off, he found a job in his own area that was most satisfying. Similarly, another person mentioned being terminated from a job in a cramped, regimented office—an environment which she detested. She needs room to operate.

Most felt that as they progressed from one age group to another, their goals became more focused; thus, career changes were less traumatic and adjustments were easier to make. As one respondent said, "I found if I stuck to what I knew and improved my knowledge in my own field, I was better off than if I ventured into a brand new unfamiliar area. This didn't mean I became stagnant, only that I used my head a bit better."

Do's and Don'ts. What did they consider the most important things to do to keep a management position? Here's one candid reply: "Do what top management says regardless of your own opinion." Other answers include: keep flexible, keep up with changes in the job, take responsibility without being reminded to do so, maintain objectivity, and keep the lines of communication open. These statements reflect their positive view of the work ethic, which influenced almost all people of this age group who are still on the job.

It's the nature perhaps of the "old" to want to pass along advice to those still struggling up the ladder. The following are lists of do's and don'ts that seem to make good sense. Remember, these came from people who have been through the mill. None are offered in a facetious manner. (My own comments are in parentheses.)

Do's
1. Make and state your objectives.
2. Request aid, from above and below.

3. Never make decisions without discussion. (Unless it's absolutely necessary.)
4. Always make a decision. (Pussyfooting can drive both supervisors and subordinates crazy.)
5. Be ready to say "no."
6. Know your boss's (subordinates' and peers') hobbies.
7. Always ask questions. Remember you are not perfect.
8. Become involved in the community—pick a tough area—and it may save your sanity.
9. Analyze, plan your progress, and work hard.
10. Have a sense of humor and keep things in perspective.
11. Study what is new—keep up.
12. Be known for your integrity.
13. Be known for your consideration.
14. Be known for your accessibility.
15. Train subordinates.
16. Check performance constantly.

Don'ts
1. Don't try to be a hero.
2. Don't assume others are looking for your job. (One could write volumes about locked briefcases and drawers, unwillingness of people to give advice, furtive glances over the shoulder.)
3. Never say "yes" to your boss unless you agree.
4. Don't say "yes" when you really mean "I don't know."
5. Don't hold the floor.
6. Don't belittle others. (Neither they nor you are perfect.)
7. Don't listen. (You're the boss.)
8. Don't send lots of memos. (Unnecessary memos will rarely help save your job. You'd better have some-

thing stronger to stand on than a few written words.)

9. Don't speak of others' concerns. (Depend on your own opinions and thoughts.)
10. Don't forget your boss's wife's name. (Or her husband's name, if your boss is female.)
11. Don't be complacent.
12. Don't play politics.
13. Don't be uninformed.
14. Don't appear unstable in anything, whether personal or business.
15. Don't discourage people from seeking your advice.
16. Don't fail to see the silver lining.
17. Don't be discouraged—keep trying.
18. Don't marry the company. (Too often working can take up an inordinate amount of time.)
19. Don't live in the past.
20. Don't expect other people to strive to please all the time.
21. Don't talk too much. (It's a temptation to reminisce or to remind everyone of how the job was done before.)

In addition, those surveyed stressed the importance of delegation, of gaining the necessary knowledge to do the job (even though you might feel embarassed about going back to school), of concentrating on changing yourself and not others, and finally, of understanding your own goals and ambitions.

Attitudes toward Work. Half the respondents voiced their opinion about certain statements pertaining to work. See Table 5 for a summary of their responses. All of them feel that job success is very important to their self-image, but less than half say that accomplishments off the job are the most important source of self-image. Half

Table 5. Statements about work in the sixties.

	Agree Strongly	Agree	Disagree	Disagree Strongly
Job success is important to my self-image.	80%	20%		
Personal accomplishments off the job are the most important source of an individual's self-image.	40%		40%	20%
Long-term career planning is difficult to achieve.		50%	30%	20%
Most people's career plans are more dreams than strategies.	20%	30%	10%	40%
Career advancement is often as much luck as strategy.		40%	30%	30%
Job satisfaction is more important than job advancement.	10%	30%	60%	
Who you know is more important than what you do.		40%	40%	20%
It's better to switch employers to gain more opportunity than to await promotion from within.		50%	30%	20%
Slow but steady advancement will get you further than job-hopping.		10%	30%	
Family or personal commitments should come before ambition.		30%	40%	
Most people have made it into the line of advancement by age 35.		30%	30%	40%

Table 5. Continued.

	Agree Strongly	Agree	Disagree	Disagree Strongly
If you haven't made the grade by age 40, you'll never make it.	10%	10%	50%	30%
Most people over 55 are more concerned with retirement than with career advancement.		30%		
Immediate superiors are the most important influences on one's advancement.	40%	50%	10%	
A spouse can make or break a career.	20%	50%	30%	
Job security is more important than job advancement.		20%	50%	30%
After one gets to be 40 or so, it's better to stay with one firm than to switch employers.		10%	50%	40%

of them agree with the statement that career plans are more a matter of dreams than of strategies. Half say that it is more advantageous to job-hop than to wait for promotion from within. Those who indicated that you have to move out to move up averaged at least three major job changes during their careers. As in my own case, each new job brought more money and more prestige.

Interestingly enough, a majority disagree with the statement that job satisfaction is more important than job advancement. Ambition and advancement, in other words, sometimes did not necessarily ensure job satisfaction. About a third say that family or personal commitments should come before advancement (I had expected more people to indicate the importance of family commitments). This serves to point out the importance that employees of this age place on work. In talking about past jobs, however, several people mentioned turning down a position in another geographic area because of school commitments of children. Another said his wife's unhappiness with the Midwest drove him back to a less lucrative job in New York. If the parents of people in this group are still living, they are often in need of help and support; those respondents who might like to retire continue working in order to provide the family with financial assistance.

Practically all of those surveyed agree that there is no disgrace in not making it before the age of 40. They say that age itself is not a marker by which you should make decisions. It is interesting to see, too, that job security is not as important as advancement, and that the age of 40 shouldn't stop you from switching employers.

A large majority indicate that a spouse can make or break a career. In spite of ever-rising divorce rates, many people, especially in this age group, still recognize the value of a long-term, stable marriage. Having had a supportive husband, I appreciate how important this factor is. To buck both the job and home would be a rough struggle.

Several individuals did not rate education as high as those in other age groups did. People in this age group are the survivors—the ones who achieved success without the formal education we now expect of every management trainee. It is interesting that even though some of these people do not rank education as essential, over half have at least two degrees. Mentor and role models were not mentioned by those who answered, but supervisors were. Most did not attribute their success to the fact that they were or were not born into the right family. They do pay tribute to their friends for their help. Personal interests and characteristics have been very important in career movement.

Conclusion. These executives are still full of vim and vigor, are proficient in their jobs, are responsible, and are active participants in the work world. They have become accustomed to management vagaries and have adjusted to them. If they lose their jobs, they are often ill-prepared to start a new career unless they can foresee the change and plan for it. Most believe that they have been successful as a result of their own hard work. However, they do attribute a good share of their success to help from others and to "being in the right spot at the right time."

Possibly because of past success, they face their future work life and retirement with optimism. Many plan to continue working in some capacity after retirement. If management phases out this skillful, highly trained, and motivated segment, then it wastes their talent and loses their productive contribution to the company.

The hazards facing people in this group include: pressure from younger workers who feel that people over 60 are no longer capable and productive; the possibility of becoming incompetent because of failure to keep current; personnel shake-ups that result from mergers or acquisitions; the threat of illness or major disaster; difficulty in obtaining another job because of age; and the possibility of taking a cut in pay if job changes must be made.

However, the situation is by no means bleak: more and

more companies are recognizing the contributions of older workers; companies are offering attractive working arrangements, such as flexible working hours; there are protective laws such as the Age Discrimination Act; and management acknowledges jobs well done. Many people over 60 have become successful in industry, have gone into business for themselves, or have taken prestigious posts in academia.

Case Study: William Fletcher, Specialist in International Labor Relations

One of the best-informed experts in international labor relations took early retirement in order to run his own show and develop a business that he will continue to manage through his "retirement" years.

He started his work career as a paper boy, then pumped gas from the age of 13 until he graduated high school. After high school, he became a machine operator in a chemical plant, where he found working conditions to be so poor that he helped unionize the plant. He left that job to become a traveling salesman for a ready-to-wear clothing firm where, in addition to selling, he helped run style shows in many towns in the Midwest. When the firm began making uniforms during World War II, he left to take a job in a machine shop. Management recognized his talents and diverted him from union organizing to a supervisory position (a path taken by several leading industrial relations directors).

His next venture involved moving from the Midwest to the East Coast when he specialized in labor relations for a large aviation company. When employment was reduced at the end of World War II, he spent several years as an executive in trade association work, always specializing in labor and industrial relations. He left this work to become the vice-president of the firm from which he retired.

He represents people of older generations who became successful without college degrees. They made every work experience worthwhile, by careful observation and just plain hard work. It pleases him to be called in as the expert by many universities and management centers. He endorses the idea of education more wholeheartedly than many who have obtained their education without stress or strain. He says it is essential to have a degree in today's work world.

He feels it is important to keep an open mind and to challenge practices that don't facilitate effective management. He is impatient with pomposity and incompetence and has left more than one job when the presence of those characteristics hampered his movement. Constant shifting of top management destroys the direction of an enterprise, according to his thinking.

He appreciates financial security, which he feels allows one the freedom to react. He admires the independence of the young, and reasons that much of it is due to their practice of challenging their professors throughout their college years. They come into a work situation and continue this practice of challenging.

Bill Fletcher is a realist and knows that the teaming of a young, educated manager with a seasoned old-timer can cause trouble unless both are attuned to the situation. The young person who insists on calling the pro "Pops" can often cause the older employee to shut up like a clam—and the new person will learn nothing. Bill mentions, too, young people who are not willing to conform to company rules on dress or even personal cleanliness. They will never be successful managers, not because they lack ability, but because they won't conform.

He also has observed that long-term, ineffective managers can eventually find spots where they can work without rocking the boat—a variation of the Peter Principle. He decries managers who personalize every situation and who insist on attacking individuals rather than the issues. That attitude has caused the downfall of many executives and should be avoided. He recognizes the political nature of the management arena and knows that sometimes competence is not the basis for management's decisions about people.

He has had to push hard to get to the top, and as a result he comes across as a shrewd individual. He is successful because he has weighed his management decisions carefully, but he couples his intelligence with deep understanding of people and respect for what they can do. His path upward has involved changes from company to company, rather than the somewhat slower route of staying with one company. He is well respected and hopefully will continue his career for many years.

Case Study: Dr. Charlie Jones, Head of the Economics Department at a Liberal Arts College

Because the path to academia offers opportunities to people over 60, the case of Dr. Jones is included as a complement to that of William Fletcher. Charlie Jones was born of German parents and grew up in the Bronx. His father and grandmother sold a cow or two in Germany to obtain passage to America, where opportunity beckoned. As the only child of hard-working people, he was imbued with the importance of both work and education. He was chosen for the wonderful Lincoln School associated with Columbia University, and became a scholar early in life. He holds degrees from Bucknell and the Wharton School of Finance. He obtained a Ph.D. from New York University at the age of 54, which reflects both his love of education and his persistence.

He served in World War II in an IBM unit in New York, covering troop movements. After the war he spent almost 20 years as a businessman in partnership with his father in the competitive wholesale food business. It was when the business climate changed drastically and his father died that he decided to get his doctorate. He received a job offer from a small but well-respected college in New York. Although he earned less than he had when he was in business, he opted for the professorship because of its different set of challenges and because he felt he had some realistic experiences to share with business majors.

He becomes frustrated with the politics and the competitive atmosphere of the college, but he enjoys much about teaching. He satisfies his business yearning by doing outside consulting. He had proved that someone over 60 can do a very competent job. His students appreciate him because he can provide them with a realistic view of what they will face when they graduate. The firms that engage his consulting services have high praise for him, too.

He proves that flexibility, scholarship, and practicality do not mysteriously vanish at the age of 60.

7

Retirement—

Crisis or Easy Transition?

Overview

"Retirement," asserted Ernest Hemingway, "is the most loathsome word in the English language." The concept of retirement has only recently became more or less accepted as the end of work life. We in America have been conditioned to look forward to the "golden" years, the "grow old with me, the best is yet to be" idea. But is it really that way?

For many, the traditional retirement age 65 or even early retirement at 62 means that gainful employment ceases. The employee in a routine job or a blue collar worker is apt to look at retirement as an escape from work. He or she leaves the job to the plaudits of peers and settles down at home, or moves to the Sun Belt to enjoy life. However, fewer professionals and managers find the forced separation from work a pleasure. They would rather keep working, and many of them do.

The graying of America is now a fact. We know that the proportion of older to younger people is increasing substantially. The U.S. Bureau of the Census predicts that there will be 40.6 million Americans (or 16.5 percent of the population) over the age of 60 by the year 2000. That's a 23 percent increase over the July 1, 1978, figure. In contrast, the population under the age of 20 is expected to decline by 10 percent by the year 2000. This means that younger workers will be supporting an increasingly larger group of senior citizens. It may be that in the future, people will be expected to work after 65.

The government has helped to foster this idea. The passage of the Amendments to the Age Discrimination Employment Act in the late 1970s permits employees to work until age 70. Mandatory retirement at age 65, which has been part of most company plans, can no longer be enforced. The same regulations apply to almost all federal and state workers—except military personnel, who cannot forcibly be retired for reasons connected with age. New York City has introduced rules which would forbid age-related forced retirement of city workers.

About 33 percent of the people who reach 65 continue to work. The Department of Labor has estimated that there are about 200,000 Americans who will keep working after 65. A recent New York Times–CBS poll (1977) found that 58 percent of those questioned would work after age 65 if they could.

Those who plan to retire at 65 or even earlier usually do so for one of three reasons: (1) Health considerations are a major factor in the decisions to take early retirement. (2) If the retirement plan is financially adequate, then the person at least considers retirement. (3) Some people feel that their own savings are substantial enough for them to quit the rat race and retire.

Changes in the mandatory retirement age have created some extra problems for management. Now, in order to get rid of an oldster, reasons other than age must be found. This means that the merits of each employee must be considered individually. Personnel practices, especially evaluations, must be sharpened. Dealing with people who are 70 or older is apt to be one of the most ticklish problems facing the managers of the future.

If older workers decide to extend their working life, they can block the advancement of younger colleagues, who will be forced to compete for higher level jobs with experienced and politically smart older employees who are reluctant to retire. This can open the door to a series of related problems, including the obstruction of affirmative action plans for hiring and promoting women and minorities and the loss of promising young employees, who may decide that changing jobs and employers is the only way they can assume greater responsibility.

Resolving these problems calls for management creativity and ingenuity. In the end, the elimination or changing of mandatory retirement is going to affect each organization differently. How the problems are handled depends on how well plans can be made. Many companies have developed flexible plans which allow workers to retire any time between the ages of 55 and 70. Some companies permit older workers to "phase out." Gradually, they work less and less as they get older. A few companies move those who are about to retire to less stressful positions.

Abandoning the myths about aging is a major step toward the goal of utilization of human talent. Developing realistic measures of the relationship between age and performance, defining abilities and skills needed for various posts, eliminating age bias from performance evaluations, and continuing to research the needs of older workers will help companies to take better advantage of their human resources. The business community can ease the transitions from work into retirement by granting sabbaticals, providing better placement services, and utilizing the experience of retirees. Wise management will react positively to the graying of American and will flexibly respond to the needs of the people in the retirement brackets.

For example, Intertek Services Corporation in Rolling Hills, California, which deals exclusively in the field of aerospace and highly technical industries, has a personnel base of formerly retired engineers. The average age of the employees is 57. They have found that these retired engineers and inspectors are more professional, more reliable, and more conscientious than the new crop of engineers. However, the firm does hire many younger people in order to handle the brand new technology.

Some banks have found that the conservative older worker who had built his reputation in the financial area is less likely to take risks and is better qualified than a young executive. A university in San Francisco where many retired scholars have found teaching positions is just another example of the utilization of retirees.

How one reacts to retirement seems more of an individual matter than any other change in work life. Some people can hardly wait to quit work so they can do the things they've dreamed of for many years: traveling, fishing, golfing, painting, charity work, visiting grandchildren. For many, however, retirement brings a feeling of being pushed out by a younger, almost brutal, force. One day a genius and the next a has-been. It's not hard to find members of this group haunting park benches, hanging around the house, trying to supervise long-neglected domestic affairs, and generally getting in everyone's way. For them, retirement "happiness" lasts for about a year. Traveling loses its attraction, paintings are not as great as expected, and they've caught up on all their reading. No one needs them anymore.

Physical well-being often becomes a matter of prime important for senior citizens. Aches and pains and Medicare are the subject of too many conversations. One's personal health habits may be of some interest to a few dear friends, also beset with every sickness in the world, but it's a bore to most of us. Comparison of operations seems to be the chief hobby of too many retired people.

Another group spends time belittling or bragging about their offspring. Again, the grandson's or grandaughter's incredible achievements may interest a few people, but the stories do wear thin. Worse are the ones who complain about their ungrateful children who don't visit, don't care about, or are just plain mean to the old folks.

Then there are the people who remember their exploits at work as though they were battlefront memoirs. The memories of winning a union election, being cited for excellence in safety, introducing a new product, or picking a brilliant subordinate are as fresh as if the events happened yesterday. And yet in the retelling they're as boring as repeated war stories, regardless of how fascinating or exciting the actual events were.

These are the sad folks. There are others who handle their retirement gracefully. In reviewing all the answers to the questionnaires, it seems that there is almost universal agreement that retirement should be planned. Many firms start retirement counseling for employees at age 60, and most executives involved in such programs speak highly of them. For those people, retirement isn't a terrible shock, but a gradual transition.

Some firms will retain an individual part-time as a consultant and let him or her phase out of the job gradually. I had that type of arrangement for three months. It helped me to realize that I really was leaving and needed to make basic decisions about what to do. It helps to come to grips with the fact of retirement as early as possible. Do you want to sit on the porch and rock? Or do you want to keep working? If so, what do you want to work at? Will your friends in industry be supportive? What about your family? Can you still have a productive work life, or will you be concerned with busy-work that has little to do with reality?

My Retirement

I could hardly believe that I was the one being touted at the retirement party. The kind words, the eulogies about my greatness, and the good wishes have somewhat of a false ring, no matter how kindly spoken. A trip to the Social Security office, where I became a number rather than a person, was a demeaning experience for me, as it is for many of yesterday's busy executives. It was hard to believe that I had reached the venerable and vulnerable age of 65.

Departing from a job where I had been happy on a day-to-day, regular basis for over nine years was an abrupt change for me. Other than being fired, it is probably the most traumatic of any other changes in work life. In my own case, I expect it was the most dramatic one since I stopped teaching school in Ohio about 50 years earlier. It was a switch from the familiar to the unfamiliar. Even though I had approached the transition with well-laid plans, it was brutal. However, I managed to survive the change.

How does the rat race look in retrospect? Some of the

things I once worried about seem somewhat insignificant: deadlines for meetings and publications, budget problems, and office politics, which mattered so much, have lost their importance.

Fortunately, two consulting firms asked me to be on their staffs. The combined income was better than I made at NRMA. With the help of Jack Sheridan and Associates from Chicago, I founded my own consulting firm. With the first year behind me, I have enough projects rolling to keep me even busier than I was in any of my past positions. Working with several industries, writing two books, running a few meetings, and teaching part-time at two colleges has made my first year of retirement an exciting time. I'm my own boss and work at a different pace than before.

What do I find encouraging? I find the acceptance of my capabilities by so many of the executives I have known over the years the most rewarding part of retirement. None seem to think that my capabilities or facilities have diminished—or if they do, they have failed to tell me so. The versatility of work that is available without too much pushing is also most encouraging. The flexibility of work time also has its advantages. For the first time last summer I was able to take two hours off during each day and went swimming. It also means being alone a lot and not having the advantage of communicating frequently with peers and other fellow executives. So for me, the advantages of "retirement" far outweigh the disadvantages.

Another side advantage that cannot be overlooked is the pleasure of seeing my husband who is also "retired and working." We both spend much time working at home. Rather than finding this arrangement draining—as it is for some wives when the husband invades the wifely domain—I find it most rewarding.

The disadvantages are there, however. The office in my home is always open. It is hard to pass it without entering if jobs are undone. I find myself sometimes working 50 to 60 hours a week. The uncertainty of whether my good luck will hold for several more years is always there. The worry about finances seldom leaves someone who worried through the depression years of the 1930s. I'm one of those who in my young teaching days went through that period. A fourth disadvantage is the lack of support staff. My assistant who was with me for 18 years is no longer at my side to help me deal with unpleasant happenings or to furnish the information she always provided.

Survey Results

What about the people in the survey? Although only two were included officially, I have talked with ten more. Three moved to Florida; one is a CPA and spends at least 20 percent of his time on the financial management of the condominium where he lives (at tax time he is very busy), and the other two sit in the sun and enjoy it. They spend their time trying to convince the rest of us to do the same.

A retired labor relations expert who negotiated about one hundred contracts a year when he was working full time is now consulting in the labor relations field. He has been retired for six years and still keeps busy. He has become chairman of the Rotary in his area and represented that club at an international meeting in Tokyo. A gentleman who retired from an ocean salvage operation maintains the distress telephone in his home and is called on for expert advice by the company from which he retired.

Another woman has "retired" to teach at a university. One person retired early because of ill-health, then mastered his infirmities, and now has a second career in consulting.

Advice from Retirees

Here is the advice these people have to offer. Analyze your situation as well as you can. Remember, if you haven't ever been a painter or done any writing, it may be a little late to learn. Find and plan work in areas you are best at. There are major projects that are suited to retirement, when time is more available than it was during the hectic days of full-time work. If you have written one book, now may be the time to write another. If you really like teaching, there are openings for experts at the university level.

Your reputation, based on your long years of experience, is probably your best key to successful work. Time is more flexible and there is a wealth of opportunities, if you look for them. However, if you haven't been successful or are not somewhat aggressive, opportunities won't fall in your lap. You must seek them out. The other very grim feature is that no matter how great your pension, the inflationary trend in the last ten years, which shows no signs of improving, has made many retirees lower their living standards and has filled their days with uncertainty.

Everyone knows that some day a decision will have to be made about really retiring and quitting work. Until that time comes, however, people with talent will probably keep on contributing to make the world of work spin around a little better and a little faster.

Case Study: Frank Carroll, Retired

Frank Carroll retired at the age of 65 because of the mandatory retirement age specified at his association. He had spent many years as a marketing expert in a large retail establishment in Texas. Because he was an entrepreneur, he then went into business for himself. Like so many small retailers, he was bought out by a large chain when he was 55. Even though he felt financially secure, he wanted to continue working. He became vice-president of marketing for a retail association. He was a great asset to the association because of his experience and his willingness to share information. He was imaginative and creative—two attributes of the successful marketing man.

His personal life impinged on his work life. He was unhappily married and opted for divorce. Although he was devoted to his children, they seemed to give him nothing but trouble. He got his real pleasure from working and traveling. Fortunately, he met an understanding woman who became his bride when they were both in their mid-sixties.

His retirement party was a pleasant occasion because he was not unhappy about leaving. He looked forward to golfing and swimming when he retired to a condominium in southern California. He does some consulting work, but only for a few chosen clients. He has mastered the secret of balancing his less hectic work life with a most pleasant existence while he is off work. His current private life is a happy one, so it looks as though retirement for him has lived up to the promise of being the golden years.

8

Management Framework

for the Future

How do the findings of the survey fit into the management framework of the 1980s? Will the young and middle-aged executives of today, who are full of hope and enthusiasm, be able to attain the goals so clearly stated in their answers to the questionnaire? Will their chances of succeeding be stymied or enhanced? How will managers in their fifties and sixties cope with the changing face of the business world?

Let's take a quick look at the work world of the future. It is estimated in a survey conducted by *Psychology Today* (May 1978) that almost 60 percent of executives and managers will change jobs within the next five years. According to this survey, the ones who are going to move are looking not only for money, but also for an opportunity to learn and grow, to exercise their talents to the fullest, to have control over the decisions that affect the job, and to control the pace of the job. Several reported that they felt trapped in their current jobs and were hoping that the next jobs would be better.

The talk about better utilization of human talents is not new. Estimates of how fully the talents of managers are

119

utilized run from a low of 10 percent to a high of 40 percent. How do you unlock this dam? Many companies are taking advantage of the computer to find the talent enmeshed in the personnel files of mammoth corporations. Not only can the computer help identify candidates, but it can furnish instant data on any deficiencies, so that the executive who is about to be appointed can get a better grasp of the future job. Computerization of information about human resources is a definite feature of the future management.

Will the better utilization of talent from within a company slow down the search for talent on the outside? Not until there is a bigger crop of competent executives to fill the increasing number of management jobs, according to the experts in recruitment and executive search. The prediction is that in the foreseeable future middle and top management jobs will be filled by recruitment from the outside in over half of the cases.

As an example, a training job which a short time ago paid $12,000 to $15,000 per year now goes begging at $35,000. There just is not enough managerial talent to go around and the talented and well-trained few are asking for and getting higher and higher salaries.

One characteristic of the current management scene is the lack of life-long loyalty to one company. Executives move, as pointed out often in this book, to new jobs where opportunity and compensation are greater. This does not mean that the executive doesn't devote full talents to the particular job at hand. He or she usually works as hard as possible to make the current employment pay off for both the individual and the company. As far as we can predict, this trend will continue.

Will the rate of mergers and acquisitions, a mixed blessing for the modern-day executive, slow down? Probably not for the next 10 or 15 years. Although it may seem that there are few companies left to merge, there are still many thousands of small enterprises yet unswallowed. The search for increased profits through mergers and acquisitions continues and, in spite of all protestations to the contrary, the shuffle in the management hierarchy will be enhanced by such moves.

Will executives assigned to new spots refuse to relocate? According to Merrill Lynch Relocation Management, Inc. (*The New York Times*, June 25, 1978), which specializes in moving executives, 200,000 to 300,000 top managers were asked to move in 1978. The study reports that one-half to one-third of them refused to move, whereas only 10 percent balked 10 years ago. The chief reason given was that the family didn't want to pull up stakes. (However, there is a growing number of long-distance marriages, in which the mother or father jets to the family home on weekends, or makes periodic visits.) Among the people included in the survey, only one refused a job because his family didn't want to move. Although some factors indicate that there will be fewer transfers in the future, the evidence of this study indicates that the way up means breaking habits of a one-area career. The ease of air travel, the urbanization of remote areas, and the growth of a restless generation have all added to the facility with which moves are made. Most managers know that if they refuse one transfer, management will probably be reluctant to offer a second or third choice. "Let's not offer that job in California to Hal, his wife will never leave New York," is apt to be management's assessment of Hal's promotability.

One of the real issues of the future is planning for two-career marriages. More and more women are entering the business and professional world. What happens when a success-oriented woman and an equally career-conscious man want to get married? Who will move or sacrifice? It can no longer be assumed that the wife is the one who will give up a lucrative, exciting job to follow the husband. Business assignments often require spending only four to ten years in one job, whereas building a profession may take a lifetime of investment in one place. Long-distance marriages are not very satisfactory to many. As I see it, this is one of the pressing problems of the 1980s. Some of the younger people in the survey voiced concern about this, but in their usual confident fashion assured me that they could work it out.

Another problem facing management and managers of the future is the delicate issue of reverse discrimination. Some young people feel they have been passed over several times for promotions or key jobs so that management can meet its legal obligation to compensate for past discrimination. Those people feel they are not being judged fairly, on their own merits. Coping judiciously with this ticklish situation will be a real challenge during the 1980s.

What other trends are emerging as we enter the 1980s? We'll certainly see more well-educated managers. Ph.D.s will no longer be a rarity in executive suites. Psychologists interested in the utilization of human talents and other facets of the business world will become more visible. Highly trained technicians will find more and more jobs as we increase our use of the computer and other specialized machines.

Rigid scheduling patterns of today may be replaced by flexible part-time arrangements for highly skilled people. People will be valued more for their know-how and their skills than they have ever been before. This may mean a

24-hour week for some specialists, who then can devote the rest of their time to research or to leisure.

We hope that the talents of the growing number of elderly people will be better utilized. We must stop regarding old people as human garbage and start respecting them as survivors of the executive jungle who have gained wisdom that can be shared with younger people. They should be regarded as heroes who have survived numberless crises and who may be able to suggest methods to avoid similar crises in the future. Much of the drive to find alternatives is coming from those in their sixties or older, who are calling on their ingenuity and courage and are refusing to be shelved.

9

Conclusions

What has the survey showed us? First, the talks with executives and the answers to the questionnaire are based on reality. These are not the reflections of a few sheltered people, isolated from the fast-moving world around us, but are the observations and insights of a dynamic group of management men and women at every age of work life. The questions have been answered with care and with openness and thus, I believe, represent a most interesting slice of today's management life.

The work ethic is extremely strong. No one complained about long hours and risk-taking; instead, the emphasis was on the job to be done and on accomplishments. "Work is real," "Work is exciting," and even, "Work is fun" were only a few remarks. "Work is the key to the good life and in itself is a way of utilizing my talents, which I enjoy" is the expression of one of the participants. These attitudes coincide with the rest of the American scene at the present time. Business is no longer the ogre some people made it out to be during the 1960s. Flower children have been replaced by the eager students anxious to enter the business world. The worst calamity feared by many an executive is the loss of employment.

Anyone who doubts this need only look at the long lines of those waiting for jobs whenever there is even a rumor that good positions are available. The waiting lists for promotions to higher level jobs are realities in most companies.

Bucking for higher paying jobs and correspondingly higher responsibility are characteristic of those who responded to the survey. Comparitively few were content with their current positions, but rather had great plans for the future. "I'm a vice-president now, which I aimed to get in my first ten years of employment at the bank. I plan to be a senior vice-president in the next five years. I'll either get it here or move where I can get it." This remark is typical of people in their late thirties.

Is there still a Horatio Alger flavor to many of the careers of those in the study? Yes, particularly among those in their later years who started from very humble beginnings or came to America as a result of troubled times somewhere else in the world. From the farms of the Midwest people have moved to executive suites in Manhattan; from the holocaust in Europe the tough survivors have tasted sweet success here; from the ghettos of our urban areas there have been spectacular success stories. As for women, the older ones now at the top made it the hard way. The young ones have an equal start with young men and are bound to do well, as witnessed in several examples in the study.

Several respondents readily admit that a network of executive friends and an education from an Ivy League school played an influential part in their success. A review of top executives shows a fair mixture of both those who made it the hard way and those who had all the early advantages. Those who made it the hard way are anxious to see that their sons and daughters start with the advantages they themselves did not have.

The restlessness of the respondents seems typical of

the times. Whether job changes are the result of a chance meeting with an old friend, a supervisor's last-minute decision about an assignment, or a personal involvement or tragedy, the resulting adjustments can have a tremendous impact on where a person lives and his or her success and personal satisfaction.

Why do people want to move up? Management jobs are no beds of roses. You are responsible not only for your own welfare, but for the welfare of those you supervise. The success of your peers and of the whole organization also may hinge on your decisions. The hours are long. Many jobs entail travel and perhaps a move for you and your family to other parts of the country or of the world. However, the satisfaction of making a worthwhile contribution plus a more lucrative paycheck counteracts the disadvantages of upward movement. What else do executives look for when they seek a change in jobs? Some of the reasons cited by the survey respondents include: new challenges, advancement opportunities, the chance to use professional skills to a greater degree, and the chance to move to an area better suited to their children's needs or with more appealing weather.

There are two paths to the top, and each person has to decide which one to take. You can stay in a company and make a slow but steady climb to the top, or you can move from one company to another in order to move up. Which is better? People who are impatient, especially young people, get tired of waiting and go the second route. Their in-house path may be blocked by a boss who is just a few years older. Most people admit that the job-hopper runs a greater risk, but remember that nothing is guaranteed in any management job.

Many people surveyed lost their jobs as a result of mergers, and others lost out when a consultant recommended a new management team. Other incumbents lost heart when they were passed over for someone with more talent. Some, of course, resent that so much that they resign and go elsewhere.

What other hazards have the people in the study faced? Here are just a few: lack of faith in a new boss, lack of management support for their projects, insufficient or incompetent staff support, shifting product markets, and inability to keep up with the times. Company politics came in for its fair share of criticism, too. Some people found that they could not function in a tightly structured organization. All of these reasons looked large when an executive recruiter offered a job that had more money and seemed to lack all the old troubles.

To dance around the executive minefield without getting blown up is a major feat. Is it worth the effort? The respondents in responsible management jobs—the survivors—said it was.

The do's and don'ts of getting and keeping a management job cut across all age groups. Some of those listed below may sound somewhat trite, but they represent the considered opinion of these highly successful executives. Here are some of their do's:

1. Select good subordinates and delegate.
2. Give controlled latitude to subordinates.
3. Know who is important to your boss.
4. Keep two steps ahead of your job descriptions.
5. Understand and train the person behind you to fill your shoes when you are promotable.
6. Give credit where credit is due. Don't take all the glory yourself.
7. Keep professionally fit.

8. Demonstrate that you are motivated to do the job and make solid contributions to the company's goals.
9. Demonstrate the ability to continue personal growth and flexibility to meet new challenges.
10. Work as a team.
11. Be fair, be firm.
12. Communicate.
13. Cooperate.
14. Most of all, be prepared to work hard and conscientiously.

On the other side of the coin, these same executives had a list of habits that really can hold you back. Here are a few:
1. Don't lie.
2. Don't stagnate.
3. Don't double deal.
4. Don't delegate improperly and forget to check.
5. Don't be a part of the gossip and rumor grapevine at work.
6. Don't drink too much.
7. Don't avoid taking chances.
8. Don't put success ahead of your ethics.
9. Don't play favorites.

What did they consider their biggest mistakes in management? Here are a few of their afterthoughts:

1. Not getting a better education when I had a chance.
2. Not starting my own business sooner.
3. Not investigating the new job more thoroughly before I accepted it.
4. Lack of commitment to job and company—too much emphasis on family and extra career development.

5. Lack of sensitivity to company politics. I believe my outspokenness has both helped and hurt me.

It is interesting to see that the executives included in the survey did not blame others for their failure. Most were generous in acknowledging support from their families, from the people (often parents) who gave them financial assistance early on, from supervisors and top executives who watched over and guided their efforts, and from outsiders (professors or other professionals) who gave them invaluable technical assistance.

In spite of some disillusionment, most put great faith in the importance of education and in continuing efforts to update management skills. Almost all the people surveyed mentioned that in management jobs technical skills are not enough. The fine art of getting people to produce takes extra know-how not found in technical books.

One cannot review these success stories without some sense of each person's tremendous motivation to get things done both for themselves and for the employer. Those who have been most successful are not the cutthroats, but the ones with a healthy respect for other people's talents and capabilities.

Do they differ according to their age groups? In spite of their many differences, there are the same basic desires and capabilities. The younger ones come in better educated and often better prepared than the oldsters who made it the hard way. It is interesting to note that there seems to be more risk-taking among people in their twenties and sixties than in the other age groups. The thirties and forties are the hard-driving years when reputations are made or broken. The fifties seem to be a scarier time to most people—they're still young enough to worry about the job and not old enough to relax. Those in their fifties seem most fit to get caught in merger nets or other catastrophies that the agile ones survive. At whatever age one either plans or is forced to change jobs, the people who face the situation and plan carefully not only land on their feet, but end up with better jobs than before.

Thus, young men or women who start their work life in their early twenties have an exciting and productive life ahead. The big hang-up at that early age is their lack of experience, and perhaps the unwillingness of other managers to pay attention to their philosophic discussions about solutions to the problems of the organization. The hazards include being too hasty, forming bad work habits (such as poor attention to the job or misuse of expense accounts), and not being placed in the right spot.

The young person who successfully moves into the thirties, very often with a change of jobs, faces a different picture. Here the years are spent, just as they are in the forties, in building a reputation. Many of the hazards of this period come with the stiff competition for the favored spots. It's a time, too, of heavy family responsibilities, some of which hinder and some of which help the executives travel up the ladder.

The now-seasoned manager moves into the treacherous times of the fifties. That's when the pressures from below start taking effect. Are people in their fifties as sharp as before? Can they take the extensive travel? Can they survive the political scene? The fall-out begins and the tough ones survive. Those who survive have usually moved fairly close to or are top management.

The healthy manager in his or her sixties is probably at the peak of a career. Respected for judgment and experience, people in this group reap the rewards of a well-earned reputation. These people often retire to a less hectic work life. The hazards they face are ill health, financial difficulties, and, sometimes, unappreciative management.

Is this person typical or atypical? The people included in the survey may present a somewhat over-qualified sample of executives at every age level. If so, it should still be encouraging that there are such vital people in the work world.

In other words, the management man or woman in today's frenetic climate is still one of purpose. Most of the time he or she is satisfied with work life in spite of its hazards and frustrations. The rewards really seem worth the effort.

QUESTIONNAIRE

1. What is your current job title?_____

2. What are the duties of your job? Please describe:_____

3. Does your "job description" actually describe what you do? __Yes __No

    If yes: Are you satisfied with your duties? __Yes __No

        Would you add additional aspects to the job if you could? __Yes __No

        If yes: Describe the additional aspect you would add and why:_____

        _____

        If no: Why not?_____

    If no: How do your actual duties differ from your job description? Please

        check all that apply:

        __I do not have the authority implied in the job description.

        __I do much more than the job description implies.

        __Many of the aspects decribed simply are not "on-line" in my company.

        __Other. Please describe:_____

4. What would you say was the chief hazard of your current job in terms of...

    Performing the job?_____

    Your own career?_____

5. Would you say you are satisfied with your job? Check ONE below and comment:

    __Entirely satisfied.   __Moderately satisfied.   __Unsatisfied.

    __Quite satisfied.   __Satisfied for now.   __Would change jobs.

    Comments:_____

6. I like my job because:_____

    My job satisfies me because:_____

    My job dissatisfies me because:_____

7. Under what circumstances would you consider changing jobs?

8. Is this your first management job? __Yes __No

9. If this is not your first management job, please tell us the management positions you've held before.

Job Title	No. Years	Promotion	New Job	Reason for Change
_____	___	___	___	_____
_____	___	___	___	_____
_____	___	___	___	_____

10. How long have you held your current position? __Less than 1 year __1-3 years __4-5 years __6-7 years __More than 7 years

11. Were you promoted to your current position from within or hired from outside?

   __Hired from outside. (Please go on to questions 14-17.)

   __Promoted from within. (Please go on to questions 12 and 13.)

12. If you were promoted from within your company, is your current position a natural step upward in your functional career specialty? __Yes __No

   If yes: Which of the following characterize your promotion? Check all that apply.

   __Additional responsibility.   __Increased freedom of action.

   __More managerial activity.   __Other. Describe:_____

   If no: How would you describe your current post in comparison with your former position. Please check all that apply.

   __A radical shift for career function. Describe:_____

   __A moderate shift into an allied function. Describe:_____

   __A change of career specialty reflecting a change of personal interests.

13. Which of these factors were influential in your promotion? Check all that apply:

   __Good performance in my former position implied promotion.

   __In my former post I was hired to eventually replace this position's incumbent.

   __I took additional academic courses to qualify for the position.

   __A mentor guided me toward my present position.

   __Other. Please describe:_____

_____

(Go on to question 18.)

14. If you were hired from the outside, what factors motivated you to change

    employers? Please check any that apply:

    __Lack of opportunity to advance   __Increased job satisfaction in new
    in former job.   job.

    __Slow pace of advancement in former   __Increased potential opportunity in
    job.   new job.

    __Dissatisfaction with company   __New job more in line with talents
    policy in former job.   and interests.

    __Increased salary and benefits in   __New job offers better environment.
    new job.
                                           __New position avoids transfer.
    __Increased responsibility in new
    job.   __Other:_____

15. What was the manner in which you changed jobs? Check all that apply:

    __Laid off or discharged from old   __Was offered a new position else-
    job.   where without soliciting it.

    __Resigned and initiated a job search. __Other:_____

    __Initiated search for a new post
    while still working in former job.

16. Which of the following personnel systems or techniques were involved in your

    change of position? Check all that apply:

    __Newspaper ads.   __Personal connections.   __Professional contacts.

    __Employment agencies. __Recruiters (headhunters). __Self-promotion letters.

    __Other. Please describe:_____

17. Being hired from the outside into your present position, do you find your new

    job a natural step upward in your functional career specialty? __Yes __No

    If yes: Which of the following characterize your job change? Check all:

        __Additional responsibility.

        __More managerial activity than supervisory or "doing" functions.

        __Increased freedom of action.

        __Other. Describe:_____

    If no: How would you describe your current post in comparison with your

        former position? Please check all that apply:

        __A radical shift of career function. Describe:_____

        __A moderate career shift into an allied function. Please describe:

        _____

        __A change of career specialty due to a change of personal interests.

18. Have you ever accepted a new job or a promotion that didn't work out? __Yes __No

    If yes: Describe your problem or the circumstances:_____

19. Do you have a general career goal? __Yes __No

    If yes: Please rank the importance of the factors listed below in achieving

    your goals. Assign each a rating from 1 to 10, with 1 being least

    important and 10 being most important.

    __Obtaining a certain level of responsibility.

    __Obtaining a certain level of compensation.

    __Actualizing certain projects, such as introducing a new project.

    __Working for yourself.

    __Retirement.

    __Other. Describe:_____

    If no: What are some of the reasons that the horizon is unclear?

    _____

20. Do you have a general career strategy? __Yes __No __Only vaguely

    Comments:_____

21. Can you identify what your next step might be? __Yes __No __Uncertain

22. Can you envision additional steps in your career beyond your next possible

    position? __Yes __No __Uncertain Comments:_____

23. What factors will affect your next position? Check all that apply:

    Professional factors

    __Company growth.

    __Obtaining additional education or skills.

    __Obtaining additional experience.

    __Advancement of those ahead of me.

    __Other. Describe:_____

    Personal factors

    __My age.   __My spouse's career.

    __My sex.   __Other. Describe:_____

    __My home situation.   _____

    __My personal lifestyle.

24. How important would you say each of the following has been in your career?

	Very Important	Important	Unimportant
Education	___	___	___
Upbringing and friends	___	___	___
Marriage and family	___	___	___
Mentors or role models	___	___	___
Supervisors or superiors	___	___	___
Personal interests	___	___	___
Mergers and acquisitions	___	___	___
Other:_____	___	___	___

25. To what extent would you agree or disagree with the following statements?

	Agree Strongly	Agree	Disagree	Disagree Strongly
Job success is important to my self-image	___	___	___	___
Personal accomplishemnts off the job are the most important source of an individual's self-image	___	___	___	___
Long-term career planning is difficult to achieve	___	___	___	___
Most people's career plans are more dreams than strategies	___	___	___	___
Career advancement is often as much luck as strategy	___	___	___	___
Job satisfaction is more important than job advancement	___	___	___	___
Who you know is more important than what you do	___	___	___	___
It's better to switch employers to gain more opportunity than to await promotion from within	___	___	___	___
Slow but steady advancement will get you further than job-hopping	___	___	___	___
Family or personal commitments should come before ambition	___	___	___	___
Most people have made it into the line of advancement by age 35	___	___	___	___
If you haven't made the grade by age 40 you'll never make it	___	___	___	___

	Agree Strongly	Agree	Disagree	Disagree Strongly
Most people over 55 are more concerned with retirement than with career advancement	___	___	___	___
Immediate superiors are the most important influence on one's advancement	___	___	___	___
A spouse can make or break a career	___	___	___	___
Job security is more important than job advancement	___	___	___	___
After one gets to be 40 or so, it's better to stay with one firm than to switch employers	___	___	___	___

26. What do you consider the most important things to do to get and keep a management position?_____

27. What do you consider the most important pitfalls in getting and keeping a management position?_____

28. What do you consider your greatest career achievement?_____

29. What do you consider your gravest career mistake?_____

30. What level best describes your function and title?

    __Top management __Middle management __Supervisor __Technical or professional

31. What is your sex? __Male __Female

32. What is your age? __20 to 30 __31 to 35 __36 to 40 __41 to 45

    __46 to 50 __51 to 55 __56 to 60 __Over 60

33. How would you describe your present position and attitudes in terms of career?

    (For example, "just launched," "entering maturity," "getting into stride," and

    so on.)_____

Thank you for answering the questionnaire. All answers will be kept strictly confidential and will be presented only as a part of the statistics emerging from the responses of the survey. We assure you complete anonymity, but would appreciate being able to contact you for a follow-up interview.

Name_____Title_____

Street Address_____

City, State, Zip_____

Telephone_____

INDEX

A

AAIM (American Association of Industrial Management), 57, 75-77
Age Discrimination Act, 105, 110
Alger, Horatio, 126
AMA (American Management Associations), 56-57, 75
American Association of Industrial Management (AAIM), 57, 75
American Management Associations (AMA), 56-57, 75
attitudes of managers, 15, 90-91
  toward age, 64
  toward work, 100-104
attrition, 72
authority of older manager, 92

B

blueprint for action, 12
Bowling Green University, 17
Bureau of Labor Statistics, 5, 37

C

career changes
  advice about, 83-84
  concerns about, 81
  pros and cons of, 78
  reasons for, 41, 63-64, 78-79
career goals, 20, 42, 78
career opportunities, 2

PERT (Program Evaluation and Review
    Technique), 28
Peter Principle, 85
planning, career, 53, 79
priorities, assessment of, 12
Program Evaluation and Review Technique
    (PERT), 28
Psychology Today, 2-3, 119

Q

questionnaire
    exploring successful managers, 1-2, 133-138
    results of, 18-19, 39-40, 58-60, 71-78, 95-96,
        116

R

retirees, advice from 117
retirement, 109
    mandatory, 110-111
reverse discrimination, 122
risk taking as managerial trait, 10

S

scandal, as management hazard, 9
self-evaluation, 34-35
spouse, as career factor, 103
Standard & Poor's Register, 34
success, factors influencing, 43
support, as career factor, 40-41
survival kit, for managers, 10-11

T

turning points
    of the sixties, 97-98